THE FIGHTS WE FOUGHT
HAVE BROUGHT US HERE

THE FIGHTS WE FOUGHT HAVE BROUGHT US HERE

PERSIA ARCHIE-SMITH

ANIIA D. CHERRY

NAUDIA M. GREEN

PAOLA JIMENEZ MORA

SYLVIA D. LONTZ

HALIMA OMAR

SORAYA ROBINSON

MELISA TORRES ROJAS

NATALIA UNSELD

CRAIG WRIGHT JR.

LOUISVILLE STORY PROGRAM

Louisville Story Program
851 South 4ᵗʰ Street
Louisville, KY 40203

www.louisvillestoryprogram.org

ISBN 978-0-9914765-7-2
Library of Congress Control Number: 2020945286

Edited by Joe Manning
Book design by Shellee Marie Jones
Cover art by Norman Spencer

CONTENTS

INTRODUCTION

In the past 138 years, across four locations, and through periods of immense social change, Central High School has served as a mooring point whose significance and legacy in Louisville cannot be overstated. Central alums have positioned themselves at regular intervals in Louisville's history as sentinels of our greatest aspirations for dignity, justice, and inclusion, and have beaten a path so that we all might find our way with a little more certainty. These are big fights, to be sure, which have been fought out in the open—in the streets, in the courtroom, in the lecture hall, or in the ring. Other fights are won and lost on our own, without a word, though, until we decide to tell a story and share them.

One of the primary goals of our programming at LSP is to provide our participant authors with the resources, time, and guidance required to investigate the ways their experiences have shaped them, to discover where they've been, how they got here, and what they want to say about their journey. As is always the case, a story needs two participants: someone telling and someone listening. So the other primary aim of our programming is to introduce the authors, as representatives of their immediate communities, to a thoughtful, engaged readership. Their intimate invitation to the broader community allows us to know one another with a little more clarity, and, perhaps, see ourselves reflected in their stories.

During the 2019-2020 school year, Louisville Story Program partnered with Central High and long-time faculty member Ann Walsh to provide a two-semester-long, college-level creative writing workshop. Ten authors from many different geographic and cultural backgrounds showed up and put their heads down for what was, without a doubt, the most rigorous writing they'd ever undertaken. By their accounting, it also involved some of the deepest self-evaluation they'd ever been encouraged to do. Some authors came to this project with a clear vision for the stories they needed to tell—for instance, the trauma of losing a parent to incarceration and the decade it took to repair that loss, or the long-lasting impact of war and separation from family. Other authors arrived at their narrative within the writing process itself by sifting through their own recollections, feeling around in the dark. In workshopping their ideas, they discovered the stories that were most pressing to them and worked to hone them into stories contending with issues of mental health, housing upheaval, or domestic violence.

Struggle is universal, and our community has certainly had its share. 2020 has not been easy. There was a pandemic which required widespread isolation just as the most significant civil rights movement in a lifetime spread across the globe and demanded action. Louisville was a fixture at the center of the tumult. After seventy in-class workshops, it became clear that the authors would not be returning to school and that they would have to undertake the final, most rigorous creative push in the book-writing process from a distance. For months after the school year closed, as they contended with a world that was drastically changing right in front of them, the authors continued to work. In emails, phone conversations, text threads, and physically distanced in-person meetings with their editors, they completed the chapters anthologized between these covers. When you read this book, when you come to recognize the depth of character these authors possess, when you see your own strength in their efforts and their triumphs, you'll not be surprised that they completed this truly significant and difficult undertaking under hard circumstances. These authors have the spirit of fighters in them, and their work speaks for itself. In *The Fights We've Fought Have Brought Us Here* they stand to be counted and heard. They've generously offered their experiences to us here because we're stronger when we recognize ourselves in our neighbors. We are more decent and dignified when we stand shoulder to shoulder, and when our fights are not fought alone.

—Joe Manning

CRAIG
WRIGHT JR.

THE LESSON AT THE BOTTOM OF THE HILL

Bad things usually didn't happen to me. I was a very lucky kid when I was younger, even spoiled. If bad things did happen, I was usually able to put a positive spin on them and to see the rainbow after the thunderstorm. But not this time. For me, it was a normal day. I had just left recess and was heading home on the bus where I sat with my friends and played Beyblades. I loved this game: the spinning tops hitting each other to determine who was superior among me and my friends. I always got home kind of late because I was one of the last stops, but my mom was always there to pick me up. This time when I got off the bus she wasn't there, though. My bus stop was a two-minute walk from my house, so I thought, "Whatever. I'll just walk home alone." As I turned the corner and saw my house I noticed that my dad's car was missing. I figured he was at work or over at my granny's.

I rang the doorbell and waited for my mother to open the door, waiting to see her bright, smiling face, and the usual "how was school?" When the door opened, I was not greeted with the smiling face my mother usually had, but with a face my mother had never made, like a cloud of sadness was smothering her. "What's wrong, Mommy?" I asked her. Her eyes were all red and puffy and her face was soaked from fresh tears. "Dad might not be home for a little while," she said softly. I knew something was wrong but I didn't want to push it. I never liked to see my mother sad. I couldn't stand the thought of it. I only wanted her to be happy and be the smiling mother that she always was, but at this moment she wasn't. I was lost as to what to do or say.

It wasn't unusual for Dad to go away for days at a time, so instead of asking more questions I just smiled and said, "Okay, I'll just wait for him to get back like normal." She sighed, knowing that I didn't really get what was going on and that the heaviness of the words she spoke were lost on me. "No, he won't be home for a long time. But just know he still loves you," she said, trying to keep her tears hidden from my view. I paused and thought about it. "You mean like a month? I can wait that long because I love him a lot and I know he will come back." I smiled at her, gave her a big hug, and went to my room. I hated seeing my mother like this.

Over the next few months, my mom just told me that he would be gone longer than usual. She never gave me an exact date. She was always dodging the question or changing the subject as soon as I brought it up. I didn't know that he wouldn't be returning for up to a decade. I would hear adults whispering and then the room would always go silent when I arrived, as if my presence was sucking the volume out of their voices. After a few months of waiting, it finally clicked in my seven-year-old brain that he was in jail. I walked into my mom's room and said, "Has Daddy gone away because he is in jail for doing something bad?" She pulled me in close for a hug and started to show those hidden tears. It was all the confirmation that I needed. The thought that had been lingering in my mind was correct.

At first, I didn't want to believe it. I thought, "No. Not my dad. He never does anything wrong." He was the best father anyone could ask for. He took care of the people around him and made sure that everybody was always doing good. He was always a very happy person, always smiling, and laughing, and joking around with me. He was outgoing, talking to anyone that he could. But there was another side to this coin, a side that I never knew about or even got to see. My dad would never show this side to his children or anyone he cared about. The only time I got to see even a glimpse of this side is when he was taken away.

Every day, I came closer to accepting the fact that he was gone, but I knew that even on my deathbed I would never truly accept it. It was very hard for me because my father and I were very close. He was always very family-oriented, always putting his family first and always spoiling me, though not without making me work for it first. Like the time they announced the new PlayStation 2 was coming out and I bugged him for days, asking him for it every chance I got.

"Well, how bad do you want this PlayStation?" he asked. I told him, "I want it really bad. It has one of my favorite games. I'll do anything for it."

"All right. If you'll do anything, then I want you to make a list of why you should get it and I want you to keep your room clean and do your homework. If you can do that, a month from now you'll have your PlayStation." I eagerly ran to my room and got my calendar down. I quickly scribbled my chores down on a piece of paper. *Make up my bed, make sure clothes are folded,* and *make sure I iron my clothes for school* were just a few of them. I handed my dad the calendar, paper, and pen and he flipped the page. "All right, here's one month from today. If you keep your end up, I'll keep my end up." He marked down the day with the pen and we shook hands, making the deal official.

Every day—without a doubt—for a month straight, I cleaned up my room and did all my homework. At the end of every day, I would cross off the day and count how many more days were left. The last week seemed to drag on forever but on the last day, just like he said, there was a new PlayStation sitting on my bed waiting for me when I got home.

"You did a good job, boy. I didn't expect you to pull through, but you really showed me." With a happy and shocked expression I looked at him and said, "Can I keep it? Do I really get to keep it? Is it really all mine?"

"Ha-ha. Yes, yes. It's yours to keep as long as you keep your room clean and stay on top of your homework." I was so excited to open it. I would have agreed to anything he told me.

No matter what the situation, he always tried to get me to take something out of it. I learned a lot of things about responsibility from him. He was my role model. I looked up to him and tried to be like him. I would try to do everything he did. I already looked like him. I was like his clone. We even had the same name, so it was like it was destiny for us to be close.

He had taught me so many things before he left. He was very big on respect and taught me how to treat people the right way. He would take me almost anywhere he would go, even if it was just to walk and talk. I'd be right there by his side. The two of us were inseparable. Then, like a snowflake falling into a river, it was all gone instantly without so much as a goodbye. The man I saw as my hero, the man who was always there for me, had dematerialized out of my life in an instant. Just like a boomerang thrown out of sight, all I could do is wait and hope he returned.

It opened up a void in our family that we would not be able to fill. No matter how normal we pretended to be, things just wouldn't be the same without him.

***

Once I finally put two and two together I was sad, but I feel like part of me already knew, and so I didn't get full-on depressed. After about a year or two, I became more numb to the feeling of him being gone. I still missed him, but I tried to push it out of my mind by focusing on anything but that. I tried to focus more on my school work and my after school hobbies. For most of the time he was absent, I tried to push it out, to ignore it, to not show how I was feeling. But sometimes it got to me. One night I walked past my little

a hole in my heart that only he could fill. Sure, we called and wrote letters back and forth, but it was never the same as him actually being there in person. I wanted to hear the words he wrote come from his mouth. Even around the house things didn't feel the same. There was no more, "Hey Dad, are we going over to Granny's today?" There was no more, "What are we doing today?" There was no more, "Can we have McDonald's for dinner?" Because there was no more him. The house I lived in no longer felt like my home without him in it. You never realize how much you miss the little meaningless conversations or arguments with a person until you can't have them anymore. The worst part was we couldn't even talk every day. He was in a jail three hours away, which meant we couldn't visit much either, and when we did get to visit him it would always feel off.

sister's room and heard crying, so I walked in and in my softest voice I asked, "Hey Z, what's wrong with you?" She looked at me with tears in her eyes and said, "I miss Daddy," then started crying even harder. I walked up to her and held her while she cried in my arms. "We all miss him," I said, trying to hold back my tears. "It's okay, Z. He will be back eventually," I said as a few tears ran down my face. I patted her head gently while she wept in my arms. Eventually, my mom heard her and came in and asked what was wrong. After I told her, she just held us both for a while, and we all just lay in the bed comforting each other.

While my mom did a great job of raising me on her own, the wisdom of things that only a father and his son could talk about was lost to me. Regardless of how much I wanted to forget about it, I always felt an emptiness because he wasn't there. There was

The process of visiting him was so slow and would take hours. We would have to leave early in the morning, and the ride was always terrible because of the mix of emotions in the car. It was as if we had all lost a very close loved one, and even the radio was playing the sad music of missing someone and being heartbroken. The conversations the night before and in the morning were always the same between me and my mom. "Make sure you have everything charging, including your phone and DVD player." "Yeah, I got everything together and I'm making sure it's charging now." I scrambled to make sure all my electronics were charging and that my movie was in my DVD player. My favorite movie, *The Bridge to Terabithia*, was in it. In the movie, the main character meets the new girl at school. He starts off not liking her because she beats him in a race, but they eventually become friends. As they grow more of a connection they build a treehouse together that they name Terabithia. It's only accessible by swinging on a rope over a shallow stream. The two friends have an argument and the girl storms off. After a few days of not seeing her, he finds out that she died trying to cross the bridge by herself after they promised to never go there alone. Before he even knew it, she was gone in an instant, leaving without so much as a goodbye. I have watched that movie at least twenty times. Every time I know the ending, and every time I hope that it will change, that he will go with her this time, or that she won't go by herself and will be okay. But the movie always ends the same way, with her gone and him all alone. As I got my stuff together for the trip to visit my dad, I knew that tomorrow I would watch the movie again, hoping for a better ending, not just in the movie, but in my life too.

Make sure you go to bed at a decent time so you don't fall asleep while we're visiting him tomorrow, I would always say to myself, knowing that I would be restless that night with anticipation. No matter how hard I tried I could never just go to sleep. I would have to exhaust or distract myself until I could fall asleep.

There were plenty of nights when I would be up late and start tearing up or even crying just because it didn't feel the same without him there. I would try to think back to all the good times, like the all the times my dad and I went fishing at the same green-tinted pond. Before we left, we always made sure we had everything together and that nothing was left out, and then my mom checked us over again in case we forgot something, which happened more times than not.

While I don't remember how to get there, I remember the location as if it were my second home when I was little. It was this big open pond away from any type of civilization, with a giant tree on the right side of the pond with some of its roots still exposed. The pond was kind of murky. You were able to see the surface and a few feet down into it, but even that had a very green tint to it due to all of the algae in the pond. It was very quiet without the usual constant buzz of machines or the zoom of cars passing by. Just the sounds of insects buzzing, birds chirping, and a son and father bonding and learning how to be patient. My dad showed me how to bait a fishing hook, but it took me a little minute to get the hang of it. I would get frustrated and say I was going to quit, but my dad never lost his patience with me. He just let me try until I eventually got it.

I watched as the hook sank into the murky water, swallowed whole by the dirty pond. We waited for a while, and then, out of nowhere, I got a bite. My dad had told me beforehand that he would only help me with baiting the hook and getting me out of the water if I fell in, so it was all up to me to reel the fish in. I used the technique he showed me to start reeling it in. The fish was really heavy but didn't seem like it was fighting back. The more I reeled it in, the heavier it seemed to get. My dad said that it was probably a turtle shell. I got it close enough to bring it in and claim my reward and I saw it: a rock covered in algae. Somehow the hook got wrapped up in the algae around the rock. We were amazed. My dad looked at me and said, "Boy, I've been fishing for many years, but I have never seen anyone catch a rock

before. Now this time let's try to catch an actual fish." We both started laughing.

I put on a new bait and we waited forever before the murky water shifted and I finally got a real bite. I knew this one was real because it actually put up a fight. My dad coached me this time. "Take deep breaths and guide the fish to where you want to go. Don't yank it or the hook might tear out of its mouth, but don't be too gentle or the fish will never go where you want it. You have to find a balance between everything."

It applies to a lot more than fishing, too. My dad always taught me how to be balanced and how to manage everything being thrown at me. Dad was always patient and a great teacher. He'd push me out of my comfort zone just enough for me to learn but not enough for me to get pushed away from whatever he was teaching me. He corrected me and let me try again and this really helped me. Thinking back now, he is the reason I can be so patient with people and why I'm so down to earth. He was patient enough to wait until I finally got the hang of it and didn't need his help.

But in the heat of the moment, all I could think about was reeling this fish in. I inched it in closer and closer to me until I could just reel it in and then my dad said, "Go for it," so I started to reel it in like a madman and finally, at last, I caught it. The fish was small, no bigger than a few inches, but to me that was a big achievement. I was proud that I had done it by myself. "Dad, I actually caught one! Did you see it? Did you see it?" I said, jumping up and down excitedly. He looked at me and said, "One day when you're older we can go and catch bigger fish."

We would wake up early in the morning in a frantic rush. We always tried to leave early so that we'd get as much visit time as possible with Dad. To make sure we were organized and ready for the road ahead, our morning conversations consisted of a checklist. "Do you have everything? Make sure you check your list. Come on, we need to hurry up."

With the slam of the car door there was a mix of glee, frustration, and anxiousness in the air hovering above all of our heads. The bittersweet feelings of these moments are still fresh in my mind.

My mom tried to lighten the mood in the car by telling jokes and asking us if we were excited to see him, but like a stubborn kid in the store, our emotions remained unmoved until they were ready to move, and that time was usually not until we arrived.

The Manchester facility was very plain, like any other building you would walk or drive past. But the feeling that the area gave off was anything but plain. The closer you got, a feeling of dread—of years of wasted lives—started to manifest. It was different than anything I had experienced before. It was like the building itself was designed to break a person's mind instead of reforming them, and inside wasn't any better. The feeling inside was heavy, like a weight had just been put on your shoulders, like something was grabbing onto your lungs and suffocating the slightest ounce of oxygen out. Everything was either gray, white, black, or tan. The lack of color sucked the life and emotion out of everything that entered the building. The silence was deafening.

We came into this large open room that was mostly empty except for a few blue lockers where families could put away belongings that were not prohibited. The lockers all had numbers that were either faded with time or from overuse from previous families. There was a desk right in the middle with metal detectors on each side, and one of the many guards inspected us with a slight pat-down before we went through the metal detector. The process was tedious and stupid. They had a lot of rules. The only type of electronics we could have were phones, but we had to lock them up before we could see him. Also, no tan or brown clothes. I found that weird, but I realized we couldn't wear these colors because those are the colors that the inmates had to wear. That rule was ingrained into my mind when I showed up one time wearing khaki pants. They wouldn't let us in.

"I'm sorry ma'am, but he can't wear any tan or khaki clothes in the visiting area."

"Why not? He's just a kid and he doesn't have anything on him."

"I'm sorry, but that's the policy here. You can either change his clothes or come back on another visiting day."

"Is there any way that we can see him if we didn't bring any change of clothes?"

"Well, there is a Dollar General and Walmart about twenty minutes away. You could go get him more clothes and we would be able to wait for you."

"Fine, we will be back, then."

We had to drive to a store thirty minutes away to buy some different pants. Once we got the correct clothes for me, we all got checked and were able to go in.

We got to the long hallway with an open view of the prison courtyard, which was always empty—I wondered if it was because they wanted to keep the facade of happiness together by not intimidating the families. In a small room right before the visiting area they briefed us on what to do and what not to do. This whole process had taken at least an hour to get through. "I'm going to have to make sure nobody has any electronics or watches on them, and if they do, then please put them in this box. We will give them back at the end of the visit." After about ten more minutes of the guard droning on about not getting up when we see him and refraining from moving too much and about a hundred more rules, we were finally able to get into the room where we could see my dad.

The visiting room did not match the rest of the building. The whole room just had a whole other vibe.

It was a world of color in a universe of gray. There were no plain white walls. All of them were filled with some type of color or character or background. It looked like they had modeled it after a daycare. Mickey Mouse, Minnie Mouse, Goofy, Donald Duck, and a whole bunch of different characters all danced around the blue, pink, and purple walls. The reunited families inside that area were all smiling and happy. There was a TV playing kids' shows to distract the little kids and keep them entertained, just like at their homes. The atmosphere was friendly, so friendly it almost seemed fake, like it was fabricated by a child's imagination, designed to hide the despair that floated around the air, holding everyone's lungs hostage. It's like they wanted you to forget that you were a prisoner and think that you were a guest there instead.

Once we were inside this room we had to wait as they filed in one by one wearing dingy tan uniforms. I remember the anticipation building as every person walked out the door. I would look and think, "Is that him? No, that's not him." Finally, he walked out and the smile on my face grew. "Mom, is that him? Is that really my dad?" Before she could answer I was already up and out of the chair, running to give him a hug.

"Hey, big dog! What have you been up to?" With the biggest smile a ten-year-old could have, I said, "Nothing much, Daddy." The happiness I felt to be in his arms again was the best thing ever. My hidden tears started to show. They didn't stream down my face, but they built up like floodwater in a dam. I sucked them back in and just kept hugging him. I felt safe in his arms. Everything was okay at that moment. I was where I truly belonged: right there next to my dad. I was on top of the world. We stood there for a while just soaking in the feeling

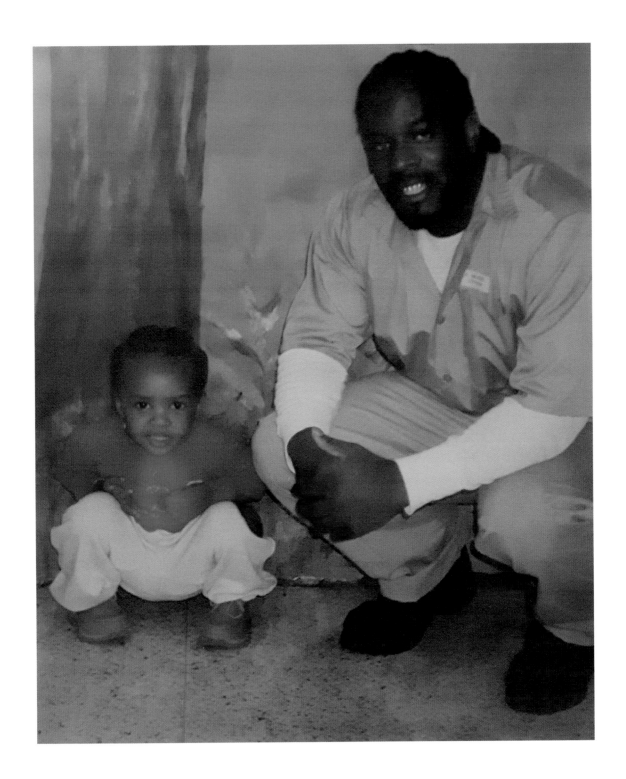

I never left that place feeling more satisfied or happier. I always felt empty, like I had forgotten something.

of finally being together for real this time. We just couldn't stop smiling.

When we sat down I finally got a good look at him. He had a few more gray hairs, but other than that he was the same happy father I had always known. The father who was always there for me and would always pick me up if I fell down. But it felt kind of awkward. Something just felt off to me. My dad and I had always gone places and talked as we traveled. Being contained in that room also contained our conversations; we never could talk about deep subjects and we never had the privacy of just father and son time. So we just had casual conversations, never as heartfelt or real as when he was at home. Sure, we were talking, and I was happy to see him, but every time I looked around I realized this wasn't home, that he couldn't go home with us, and eventually we would have to leave him again.

I watched sadly as the clock counted down and the time when we had to leave drew near. When it was time to go we said our goodbyes and headed on our way home. I never left that place feeling more satisfied or happier. I always felt empty, like I had forgotten something. But I knew that no matter how much I wanted to, I couldn't bring him home with me. I always tried to sleep on the car ride home to avoid my mom's questions. Instead of helping, the visits only made me want to be around my father more.

My dad and I were like two peas in a pod. Wherever he went I was never too far behind. The only time I wasn't with him was when he was at work or I was asleep. I met a lot of people from being around my dad. To this day I have people I don't recognize coming up to me saying, "Aren't you Craig's boy? I remember you when you were just an itty-bitty thing."

He taught me how to ride a bike and how to bait a line, but my favorite memory with him was going down a big hill.

We were riding around and talking like we normally did, but this time we took a different route than usual. We got to a really big hill with a steep decline and we stopped and looked at each other. A big smile came across my face. "Hey Dad, are you thinking what I'm thinking?"

He looked at me and said, "Are you sure you want to do that? It's a pretty big hill."

With the biggest smile on my face and determination in my eyes, I said, "Of course I do."

"All I'm going to say is be careful."

I zoomed down the hill at top speed, the wind blowing through my hair, the biggest smile on my face, and the sound of my bicycle wheels struggling to keep up. I realized it was time to stop. I tried to hit my brakes, but they did little to slow me down. My palms started to sweat. The only thing I could rationally think of in my six-year-old mind was, *Hit the brakes super hard.* So I gathered all the strength I could and squeezed the handlebar brakes. I flew off the bike, hands flailing in the air as I headed for the ground.

After going airborne, everything around me slowed down. I hit the ground hard and it knocked the breath right out of me. Surprisingly for how hard

I had fallen, I had only minor cuts and no permanent bruises, but it hurt really bad at the time. I was lying on the ground and a few seconds later my dad was over me. I wasn't crying a lot. I wanted to show my dad how tough I was. He was concerned at first but after he found out I was okay he started to laugh.

"Hey, are you all right? You hit the ground pretty hard."

"Yeah, I'm all good. Even though it does hurt, I'm a big boy and didn't cry."

"Yep, you sure are, and the way you flew through the air I'm pretty sure you earned your wings."

"What does that mean?"

"The way you flew through the air was like you had wings on your back."

"Wait, really?"

"Yes, really. Now let's get you home."

We headed home and I couldn't wait to tell my mom what had happened. "Mommy, guess what? I earned my wings today."

"And how did you do that, CJ?"

"Well, there was this big hill, and I was on my bike, and I was zooming down the hill, but I was going too fast, so I tried to stop, but I couldn't, so I hit the brakes really hard and I flew through the air and hit the ground, but I'm okay."

She stopped for a second and processed what I had said, then asked, "And where was your dad during all of this?"

"Well, he was there and he told me I earned my wings and then we came home."

She called my dad in the room. "So what's CJ talking about when he says he earned his wings?"

"Well, he went down a hill and earned his wings and took it like a big boy."

She looked over at me and I was just a smiling innocent child excited about my new big achievement. She sighed and said, "All right, as long as he is okay."

The older I got, the more I put up a wall around myself and refused to let the old memories flood over. I didn't want to forget my dad, I just wanted to forget that he was gone and wasn't there to influence me and direct me in my life, to help me grow and give me advice. I tried to not think about the situation with my dad, and for the most part it worked.

I didn't want my situation to define me, so instead of using it as an excuse, I used it as a source of motivation. I chose to learn from my father's situation. I knew that I didn't want to put my kids in that situation, so I decided to educate myself as much as possible. I was always doing research or reading up on something. I got into computers and how different electronics work. I would constantly take apart old phones and see how they worked and what made them tick. One project that I did was trying to fix a radio-controlled airplane. I took it apart and it had two different motors. Because I lacked all the pieces, I decided to build an RC car instead. I stripped the stuff from the plane and one of my old broken RC cars and I started messing around with the components. I eventually managed to replace the motors from the old car with the new plane motors and some botched wiring and it worked. Back then

I used a lot of stuff to keep me busy and distract me from the fact that my dad wasn't here. I knew that if I thought about it, it would be like opening Pandora's box, letting out a whirlwind of emotions that I was not ready to deal with.

I started slacking off a lot in middle school. It was never because I didn't understand. I either didn't do my schoolwork or I would not turn it in. I slept more in class. But I never failed a test, so my teachers knew that I knew the work. My mom and my teachers had many conferences and phone calls during this time. My mom constantly got on me, but I was never able to care about school at that point. I just lost all my motivation. My mom and teachers didn't know what to do. I eventually started getting my grades up when report cards came out so I wouldn't always stay grounded.

In middle school I was a very outgoing, friendly person. I talked to a lot of people in my grade, and everyone knew me. About a month into sixth grade, we got a new student. A new student was always fun and exciting, but a new student in an AP class really never happened. I wasn't there on the day he introduced himself, so when I came back I had no idea who he was. I was excited to talk to him, but I always made sure to observe people before I talked to them so I could know the best way to approach them. The new kid was quiet, mysterious, and didn't interact with people, which didn't give me much to work with. But it gave a strange and alluring aura to him.

He was tall and dark-skinned with a really big forehead. When I first spoke with him it was like talking to an automated machine. I walked up to his desk a little bit before class started. "Hey, my name is Craig. What's yours?"

"My name is Qua'ron," he said without looking up.

"What made you come here?"

"Reasons."

"What reasons?"

"My reasons," he said very dryly.

I thought maybe he was shy. Maybe he would be more comfortable texting. Maybe that would feel less confrontational. I said, "Hey, do you have a Kik?" which was a messaging app we all used in middle school instead of actual texting. He thought about it and begrudgingly said yes. He gave me his Kik and later that day I messaged him. As I expected, he was a little more comfortable on the phone. I went to work trying to figure out why he was so closed off and why he was so unfeeling. Over the next few weeks I started getting to know him better and became his friend.

It started with the awkward hellos and how-are-yous, then basic questions just trying to get to know each other better. I made sure that we texted every day, talked in school, and sat together at lunch. The turning point was a conversation we had after school one day in robotics.

"Hey, why did your mom name you Qua'ron?"

"I was named after the Muslim holy book."

"Why did she name you that when you guys aren't even Muslim?"

"Because she knew I would be great and lead people the right way someday," he said with a smile.

"Oh wow, that's really cool. My mom was going to name me Chase but luckily I got my dad's name and now I'm Craig."

"Ha-ha, why Chase? That's a dumb name."

"That's what I'm saying. Chase is a dumb name. Craig is a way better fit for me."

"Since your name is Qua'ron, is your nickname Q?"

"Yeah, that's what my family and close friends call me, so you can call me that too."

"Oh really? Thanks. My nickname is CJ because I'm a Junior. Only a few people outside my family know it. It just feels weird when other people say my nickname."

"Imma make sure I call you CJ all the time now."

"UGH, please don't."

"CJ CJ CJ."

"NOOOOOOO! Why did I have to tell you that?"

We both laughed and went back to researching how we were going to build our robot for our competition.

A little after that conversation I asked him why he had been so closed off at the beginning of our

there anymore and just bonded over stupid stuff like any two teenagers would do.

After just a few short weeks we became best friends. We always had each other's backs. We had a lot of common interests. We listened to the same music, we were both growing up in single parent households, and we both had a passion for robotics. As we worked on our robotics team after school we had a lot of deep conversations about how it felt to live in a single parent household.

"Do you ever wonder what it would be like if your dad was home?" he asked me.

"I mean, I know how it was because my dad was home when I was little, but he hasn't been for a while."

"My dad was never really home. He left when I was a baby. My mom only recently told me that he was locked up," Q said.

"Damn, dude. That must suck to find that out."

"Yeah, she didn't really want me to know."

"Yeah, my mom didn't really tell me my dad was locked up either. I had to figure it out on my own. But I know she was just trying to protect me."

Qua'ron and I both lacked a father figure or older brother figure in our lives, but we kind of became that for each other. From what most would see as a tragedy—not having both parents—we built a great friendship.

Qua'ron's father was never really in his life, but he would be getting out sometime during high school. His mother and father had split before he was born, so when his father got out he probably wouldn't be in the house living with them. Qua'ron told me he had had conversations with his dad, but that it felt like talking to a stranger.

friendship. I texted him, "Hey Q, I got a question for you." He read the message but took a while to respond. I thought he was busy, so I went ahead and started on my homework, and eventually he texted back.

"What's up, man?"

"So what was up with you at the beginning of our friendship? Why were you so iffy at the start?"

He said that his dad was in jail and he had to move because they couldn't afford the house they were in because his mom was let go from her job. I could tell he was sad and this was still a sensitive topic because it was still going on. His mom getting let go meant that he needed a new school and new friends. It was then that I told him that my dad was also not in my life because he was in jail. We talked for a while and joked about how our dads weren't

I asked him if he was happy that his dad would be out soon. He told me that he felt conflicted about it because he wanted to meet his dad and get to know him, but wondered if his dad felt the same. If so, why did he leave him? I had to agree with him on the last part. I was also conflicted about Dad coming home. I was happy he was coming home but felt that it would be weird because I hadn't seen him for such a long time and our relationship might have changed.

I knew that my dad was going to be home soon, and that he would be living with us because my parents were still together. I knew it was going to be a weird experience having him back in my life and being able to actually interact with him because back then I had no real male role model to look up to. Sure, my uncles were around and they taught me a few things, but the only real older male figure that I saw constantly and could talk to was Qua'ron. It was going to be hard for both of us to adjust to our dads getting out. We knew that it would change the dynamic of our home lives, but we knew we wouldn't let this affect our friendship.

When I did think about Dad coming home, I was always worried. *Will he be the same person as before? How has it changed him? Will he even be happy to see me? How will I react to seeing him?* I wondered how things around the house would be different. *Will it be less stressful on my mom?* I knew there would be some bumps in the road because he hadn't been there when my mom built up the system with us. He would have to find his place in the well-oiled machine that was our trio at the time. My mom was always strict with us, but she was always fair. If we did what we were supposed to do we were always rewarded, but if we didn't there would be hell to pay.

What if he gets home and he's a totally different person and my mom kicks him out? Would we have wasted ten years of our lives waiting for someone that's not that great?

While he was away, our main way of communication was letters. It wasn't the most up to date form of communication, but considering the situation, it was the fastest. I had no experience with writing letters. I was in middle school and the only experience I had with writing was writing papers for class, so writing a letter was no easy task for me. My mind went completely blank every time I went to write to him. Sometimes I got so frustrated that I tore the paper in half and had to start over. When I finally finished a letter, my mom would go to mail it off, and I'd remember something that I hadn't included in the letter. I'd be so disappointed in myself because it was a BIG deal writing to him and I wanted to make sure everything was perfect.

I kept every letter that he sent me. Over 100 letters. I cherished them. I made a deal with myself to keep all of his letters until the day he got home. Then I would get rid of them because, as much as I loved the letters, I only loved them because they were my only form of response from my dad while he was gone. I kept them all in a folder, hidden from everyone, and whenever I was sad or lonely or missed him I would read one of the letters and it would give me the motivation to keep on pushing.

One night, my mom, my sister and I were all sitting at the table eating dinner and having normal family small talk. "How was school, you two?" We both gave the same generic reply every kid gives:

I wanted them to read it and think, "Okay, maybe he is a good person."

"It was good." Then Mom casually asked, "So how do you two feel about your dad being home soon? It won't be long now at all." It had been nine or ten years. I said, "I'm pretty happy that he's coming home. I can't wait. It's been too long since me and him have actually been able to do things and go places together. I really miss him and I can't wait for him to teach me how to drive and do things together again, like going camping and fishing. But most of all I can't wait until we can all be a family again and all eat at the dinner table together." My sister chimed in and said, "Yeah, I want to do things like play with the toys together and go have fun as a family." After that it got quiet for a little minute, then I said, "Hey Mom, what do *you* think about him coming home soon?"

"Well, to be honest, I just want to be able to eat together as a family." She paused for a moment and then continued, "I need you two to do something, though. I need you two to each write a letter to the parole board telling them why you think they should let your father out. It doesn't have to be long. I just want to make sure that you both do something. And just because I said it doesn't need to be super long doesn't mean make it super short either. Just write whatever you feel is right."

The way she explained it was so simple, but doing it was a whole other story. I thought about it a lot. I only had till the end of the week to do it, and every time I tried to think of something to write my mind went blank. I was constantly thinking to myself, "If I mess this up, will he not get out? It's been ten years. What if he's not the same as I remember him?" As these thoughts kept piling into my head, the computer screen seemed to get bigger and bigger, closer and closer, as if preparing to grab me and swallow me whole.

I procrastinated till the last day, not because I didn't care, but because I didn't know what I would write. Every time I would come into my room to type it out my thoughts would be everywhere except where I needed them to be. I stared at the screen for what felt like hours as I tried to calm my negative thoughts. I would type a sentence and then delete it straight after. My mom nudged me in a way that kind of intimidated me. She said, "CJ, I need you to get on your computer and type a letter to the parole board about your dad. They need it to determine if he should be let out or if he should be kept in longer." I don't know if she realized it, but it put a lot of pressure on me. I thought, "If he served the time that they gave him, why do they need us to write a letter on why he should be free?"

After talking to my mom, it finally hit me that instead of writing the same old sob story that everyone would write, I would write about the good times he and I had had. I wanted them to read it and think, "Okay, maybe he is a good person." I talked about how we were always so close, about the time I earned my wings, and the time we went fishing and I caught a rock with my fishing rod. The letter just seemed to form itself in front of me. Instead of thinking about writing to the parole board, I decided to write as if I was trying to convince my dad to come home. When I finished, I didn't even let my mom read it. I already knew it was what I had needed to say.

I got home from school one day and saw my mom, which was strange because she usually worked the night shift and slept until eight or so.

"What are you doing up? Why aren't you asleep for work tonight?"

"Oh, I have some errands to run. I'll be back in about an hour or so. So don't forget to pick up your sister on time."

"Okay, I will pick her up like I always do," I said. "But didn't you just go shopping two days ago?"

"Yeah, but I forgot some things. I love you. Bye."

Just like that she was gone and I had forty minutes to kill until my sister got home. I watched videos on my phone so I wouldn't fall asleep on the couch. When it was time for me to go get my sister, I put my dog on the leash and we started walking. My sister's bus stop is only a two-minute walk. When my sister got off the bus, I said, "Hey, Z. How was school today?"

"It was good. How about you?"

"Can't complain. Mommy went running some errands, so we might be home alone for a bit."

"Oh, okay. But isn't that Mommy's car turning the corner now?"

I looked back and said, "Well, it sure is. Why is she stopping at the side of the street?" As soon as I said that, the passenger door flew open and a man stepped out. My sister and I stared in confusion, not

realizing what was going on. Then it clicked in our heads simultaneously, and before my brain could process what was going on my legs were already running as fast as I could down the street, dragging the dog behind me. I ran up to Dad and gave him a great big hug. My hidden tears started to show. "I missed you so much. I'm so happy that you're finally home." He laughed, and as I finally pulled away from the hug I could see that his hidden tears were starting to show too. "I'm so glad to be back with all of you. I missed you guys so much and I love you," he said.

All of it feels so long ago, but Dad just got out of jail six or seven months ago. Ever since he came back the house feels a lot less empty and it's starting to feel more like a home, like we're one happy family again.

There have been a few growing pains and kinks to iron out, though. I felt like I didn't know him when he first came home. It felt like we were trying to find where he belonged in the family dynamic. I knew that he was my dad, but I didn't know exactly what to talk about or how to act around him. It was weird having another person in the house, especially another man. Sometimes I didn't know what to say to him. When it was just us in the car there would be these very loud and awkward silences that we usually just drowned out by the radio.

As time moved on and the initial excitement of him being home drifted away, so did the awkwardness and uncertainty. For the first month or so it felt like we all were just restructuring how things worked around the family. But now it feels like he never left, and just like back when I was a kid I'm back by his side wherever he goes. He and I are still bonding like we used to. He's teaching me how to drive now and in most aspects is the same person I remember him being from when I was little. My mom always used to tell me how much I acted like Dad, and now that I see him in action on a daily basis it's undeniable. Crazy to think I act so much like someone I only knew up until the age of seven.

I know what events took place and why he got put in prison, but I don't see him any different. He is still my hero. We all have our mask that we show to different people, and the one he has always shown me is the loving, caring, patient, and protective one. I still love him and I know that he still loves me. He and I will always be together no matter the circumstance, and at the end of the day he loves me and all his family and always does what's best for us.

When I thought about writing this chapter, I had this desire to show people a peek into what it's like not living with a father and how it can really impact a family and shake their foundation. I wanted everyone, including my parents, to know how I felt, to share feelings that I had never talked about before.

I waited until my chapter was a decent length before telling my parents about it, and then I asked them to sit down with me separately so I could interview them. They both were down. I decided to do my interviews with them after they read my chapter. I wanted them to experience it instead of asking me questions about it. I wanted them to read it and think, "This is how he felt the whole time."

When I told my dad about what I'd been writing for this book, he showed interest in it right away. When my dad was reading it I noticed him wiping away a few tears at times and him doing a lot of smiling. "Man, I had forgotten all about this." he said. "I'm surprised you even remember all of this stuff. Some of it surprised me, hearing how you felt about certain things. I never would have thought."

I learned about how the only thing that kept my dad going all those years was thinking about me and my sister and watching us grow up, and of course my mom too. In that interview, I learned a lot more about my parents' relationship but I also got to learn more of his motivations, and his intentions now that he's moved back in with us. It was a real heart to heart connection between us.

I let Mom read my chapter while I set up the recording equipment and told her to ask me any questions she wanted to during the interview.

After she read it I immediately turned on my recorder and started with my introduction. We talked a lot about my mother's and father's relationship. I also learned why my mom didn't want to tell me the truth about where he was at. She was protecting me and didn't want me to be exposed to that side of things. She also said, "I never wanted to put your father down. I always wanted to put him in a positive light." In movies and television, when a father isn't there supporting the family or is in jail, the mother usually talks bad about him, but I can't remember my mom talking smack about Dad. I'm so lucky to have a family that builds each other up instead of breaking each other down. Doing those interviews really showed me how hard my mom and dad tried to keep this family together and whole, even when they were apart.

Our family had to be strong to not let this tear us apart and move past it instead. And I wouldn't change a thing. The experience we all shared only brought us closer together as a family. I'm more focused on the present and future than what's in the past.

PERSIA
ARCHIE-SMITH

ROUTINE CHECKUP BLUES

A doctor's appointment: that's all it was supposed to be. Then I could go home from a long and tiring day. But no, I ended up in the hospital, trapped and traumatized, all because of a stupid, simple, routine checkup.

My mom picked me up early, about twenty minutes before school was supposed to get out. I was already emotionally exhausted from having a mental breakdown at school and felt like I needed to cry. I told Mom how my teacher made me feel like shit because she didn't believe in me. We were in class and talking about how we were planning to pay for college, so I just wrote, *Oh, I'll get a job and save up money*. When she read what I wrote she said, "Do you think your little coins will be enough?" I was so angry.

"Yeah, I would be angry too!" my mom exclaimed. "You shouldn't say that to a student."

"Exactly!" I started to get frustrated about it again and let out little groans and felt myself wanting to cry because of how angry I was. But I stopped myself, like I always do.

I was already depressed, and the slightest things could give me a mental breakdown. Sometimes it could get so bad that I would feel like I didn't belong here. That's how I felt talking to my teacher. I kept avoiding eye contact with my mom, knowing it would make me want to cry since she was giving me an *everything-is-all-right-and-if-you-need-to-get-it-out-then-get-it-out* look. I'd been so emotional lately, and it was getting so hard to fight the tears. Water just does whatever it wants.

My depression developed when I was in fifth grade when I started losing friends and felt like I couldn't trust anyone. At the time it just felt like so much. When I entered middle school with people I didn't know, it was a scary time. I kept hanging on to my old friends from elementary school. It is an unhealthy habit I still do today. I remember looking at my old friends' social media and seeing them hanging out with new people. All my friends were friends with this one girl who I thought was so much like me, and I started to think they were trying to replace me. That's when it started. That feeling of people not needing me anymore. Like a phone: you use it, play with it, and it's always with you, but as soon as a new phone comes out or you don't like your phone anymore, you replace it.

I started to mess up my friendships on purpose so that I wasn't the one getting hurt. I started to isolate myself more, and I kept this a secret. I didn't want anyone in my life to know I was depressed. Not talking about it meant that I sank deeper and deeper into my head. I began to write in a secret journal about how I felt. I tried therapy and medicine and stopped both, which then messed up my mental and chemical balance more than before. I began to feel depressed, suicidal, and angry: a horrible combination. My mental breakdowns became frequent, and I could always tell when I was about to have one if I was paying attention. I start to get colder and even get goosebumps. I feel myself moving back into a dark space, like I am moving behind a curtain. No matter how hard I try, I always feel like I'm the problem. Even though I have recently done a lot more reflecting and keep giving myself a purpose, it

doesn't seem like it's enough. I know I'm needed, and I know this feeling isn't uncommon in our society, but I still feel alone.

The TARC pulled up. Mom and I got on like we had millions of times before. We've never had the privilege of owning a car. Sitting down in the back of the bus, I got my headphones out and put just one in so I would still be able to hear around me. I alternated between looking out the window and looking at my phone, wishing we were just going home instead of to a doctor's appointment. I wasn't even going for something important, just a checkup.

We finally made it to the doctor's office and walked into the orange, autumn-themed waiting room full of little children and their parents. I always feel like the odd one out when I'm there because I'm almost an adult but still going to a pediatrician. My mom went up to the front desk to check me in while

I sat down. She came back and gave me the clipboard to fill out.

"You're going to have to learn how to do this," she said. I sighed. The downside of growing up: doing things by yourself.

I looked at the top of the paper and wrote my name: Persia.

Growing up, my name actually made me sad because I could never find it on any cute keychains or Coke bottles like other more common names. I would feel left out and hate my name. I would always be associated with the Persian Empire, which frequently had ruthless and merciless rulers. I once read that if they had people to get rid of, they would use a technique called scaphism, in which a man who was being punished was laid on his back and sandwiched between two boats with his hands, feet, and face exposed. They'd cover his face and body in a mixture of milk and honey, would fill his mouth with the mixture to the point of nausea, and they would leave him in the sun and repeat this process every day until flies, wasps, bees, and worms ate his flesh, resulting in agonizing pain along with rotting in the sun. It is a horrible way to die, but an interesting and clever way to get rid of enemies. I would always associate this with my name ever since I learned about it, even though my mom found my name in the Bible.

Finally, we were called back into a bright orange and white room. Frosted windows let the sunlight in, but you couldn't see out except shadows of people walking by. I sat on the patient table, which made me uncomfortable because those tables make so much noise that my anxiety always gets triggered. I waited there swinging my legs, trying to keep busy on my

I know I'm needed and I know this feeling isn't uncommon in our society, but I still feel alone.

phone. My mom and I talked back and forth, trying to pass the time. It felt like forever before a University of Louisville medical student came in to do the normal boring checkup. He walked in and shook my hand and my mom's. "So how are you doing today?"

"I'm, uh, all right, I guess." I swung my legs, trying to soothe my anxiety.

"Good. That's good." The student typed up whatever he was supposed to. "How's school going?" I looked at my mom because it helped me stay focused and not panic.

"Um, well, it's going all right, I guess."

"You're in your last year, right?" The student asked with a bit of excitement.

"Yeah, thankfully. I'm ready to get out of there and just relax."

"Yeah, I know that feeling. What are your plans after school?"

"Um, well, I want to take a gap year to relax and figure myself out and maybe go to film school."

"Ooh, film school. Nice." He typed away again. I looked at my mom again. We made silly gestures to fill the silent air.

The student continued to ask the basic regular checkup questions: how was I, did I feel safe, was I eating right, getting exercise, having any medical issues.

"All right, I'm going to ask you some more personal questions." He turned to my mom "Mom, will you step out of the room, please?"

Mom got up and left the room. Then the student asked stuff like if I'm sexually active, if I've ever been sexually active, if I use any type of substances, alcohol or drugs.

"Have you ever thought about harming yourself or someone else?" I took a second to debate whether or not I should say yes. I thought, *There's nothing bad that could happen if I say yes. They can't be surprised with the medicine I'm on. It's natural to have those thoughts, right?*

"Uh." I swung my legs more, looking down and getting the courage to tell the truth. "Yes."

"Yes to which one?" he asks.

"Wanting to hurt myself," I answered.

"How often do you have these thoughts?"

Ugh, now I don't like where this is going. "Um, it used to be often before but I don't really have them much anymore."

"But you still have them?"

That's what I just said. "Yes." I don't know if I regretted it or was deeply thankful, but I beat myself up for it later.

He continued to type, writing whatever it is he was writing. I looked around the room, looking at a kid's drawing on the warm autumn orange wall. I pretended to trace the picture with my toe, in my mind, to help me not feel awkward in the silence.

"All right. I will let your mom back in and will go to your doctor."

He asked my mom to come in and, as we waited, we sat and talked about music and things we'd seen and more about what had happened in our day. She showed me different videos and posts, interesting things about the news, updates about random things—our usual routine.

We heard a knock at the door and my actual doctor finally came in. We expected her to just say the usual, get my health together by eating better, do more exercise, blah blah blah. Instead, she told us that she was worried about me and advised me to make an appointment with a psychiatrist. Then she said I should also go to the emergency room to have a mental evaluation. All I felt was anger. *Why do I need an evaluation?* I thought. *Okay, so I have suicidal thoughts. Big whoop. I'm not going to do anything. Maybe a few months ago, but I'm different now...I swear...*

After the appointment, my mom and I talked about how it made us feel, how angry we were. "I don't understand why I have to go! Like, I'm not in danger of trying anything now," I said with so much rage, but not enough to scream. I don't get angry like that often, even though I get irritated very easily. "Yo, I think we could always just like not go," I said, hoping she'd say yes.

"Unfortunately, they might've called over and so they might be waiting for us." My mom said, and she sort of froze. Later she told me that it was because she was basically having PTSD as she remembered being sent to an institution when she was seven. Once, in school, she'd drawn a picture of herself holding a gun to her head and one of herself dead on the ground. Her teacher was worried by this, and it became a whole process where she had to go to this place for mentally ill kids and kids with behavioral disorders. She was there for two and a half months. She went home on weekends, but she had to stay during the week. It was a traumatizing event for my mother, but she hadn't even really realized she was traumatized by it.

When we got to Kosair Children's Hospital we waited some more, which was annoying. My phone was dying, and being in that open space with lots of people had my anxiety up. I tried to distract myself and keep my mind off things by watching the people in the waiting room. There were cute little kids running around being annoying. My mom and I watched as this woman got a bunch of kids around the fish tank to keep them focused for a little bit so they'd calm down.

"This is RJ, and this is AJ and CJ and DJ, and oh, this one, this one is PJ," the lady said, pointing to different fish.

"This one's AJ?" One of the kids asked, pointing to a random fish.

"Yeah." The lady, going along with what her kid was saying. She looked back at the other parents and shrugged.

I was trying my hardest not to stare at people in the waiting room because I know how rude and uncomfortable it can be. I saw what I assumed to be a father and a teenage daughter who looked so sad. She was wearing a medical band and looked red in the face, as if she'd been crying. She and I kept giving each other glances. I really tried not to be noticed, but she looked like someone who had just been given hard news. The entire time, I never saw her have a phone or pull out anything to look at; she just sat there, thinking and trying to calm herself down as she was waiting. Deep down I wanted to go sit down next to her and talk, to figure out what was wrong, but I didn't have the courage for that and I felt like it would be rude. She looked like you would when you're visiting a loved one that's sick in the hospital or something. I know that look. It's how I feel on the inside when I think of my grandmother.

In 2019, my grandmother, whom I call Nana, had been in and out of the hospital like it was her new home. Her balance wasn't right, and she had been falling over and over again. When we went to see her I was aware of all the physical pain she'd been through. Her body was basically bone and skin from her having to get fluid drained off her again and again. Even though she looked rough, it seemed like it all went away the minute she saw me.

"Hey baby, come give your grandmother a hug and a kiss," she would tell me, talking in third person. I had never before realized how often she does this when she wants me to show her love and affection. I walked over to the side of her bed to give her a cautious but long and caring hug and kiss on her forehead.

"Hey, how have you been?" I knew the answer, but tried to make conversation since my social anxiety was starting to show up and mess with me.

"I've been doing all right. Just trying to get better and see what's wrong with me." My mom tried to help my nana by encouraging her to eat the food the doctors were giving her and listening and trying to be better and do better than she was. Just talking and being able to see one another was the important part. We visited for a few hours. Kept her company and tried to make her feel good. I tried to make her laugh and smile, so I danced a little just to entertain her. We talked and laughed about random things. My nana is obnoxiously random, funny, and naturally humorous.

My family is a hilarious group of people with an amazing sense of humor. I was always laughing growing up. It was as if everything was about smiling. My nana is so outgoing and confident. She can make anybody laugh, and that behavior is just contagious, passing it down to my mom and me until we are on the floor laughing until our chest hurts. That's just an everyday thing for us, and it's good therapy. Maybe that's why I was so happy all the time growing up: my family was all around me. It was a good environment to grow up in. When I was younger, we used to take daily walks at the waterfront. We took silly pictures together. I didn't know at the time how meaningful these pictures would be to me ten years later. Me being so happy, my nana in better health than she is now. Her health wasn't the greatest back then— seizures and diabetes—but I would take that over her health now any day. My nana was so much more active than she is now. She chased me and ran around, even if it wasn't for long. It's hard to not have tears soaking my face or to have a tinge of regret for taking it for granted. I know that this is about growing up and getting older, but you never really think about it much until it happens to you. It wasn't much, but just taking those walks, sitting outside, watching the people around us, and laughing was everything at that point in my life. Looking back on it, I believe when I started to see my family less, my sadness started to get stronger.

When my mom and I got home later that day and were talking about the visit, she told me how much of a difference it made for my nana when I came and visited. I'm her grandbaby and she missed me. She just

needed to see me and she felt better. It's crazy how one simple sentence made me feel like I had a purpose.

At Kosair, Mom and I finally got called to go back to a small area with four or five bedrooms, a bathroom, and a big crescent desk. Near the doorway, there was a small room, about two old telephone booths wide, with a black padded chair, a black wall-mounted landline, and small blue lockers, like the ones you see at amusement parks. They told us to put all our belongings in the lockers, even our phones, probably for our own safety.

They showed me to a room that had a wooden bed frame with a sheeted mattress in the middle of the room, a sitting chair beside it, and a TV behind hard-to-break glass—again, for our own safety.

Two older women who looked to be in their late twenties or early thirties accompanied me to a tiled bathroom with a metal toilet, a little shower, and a metal sink for which you had to press buttons for the water to come out. They were both in black scrubs. One woman had a clipboard with papers on it and had a gentle face. The other was holding the paper gowns and had a stern and serious face.

They came with me to make sure I didn't have anything under my clothes and to check for any bruising or cutting marks. I took off my shirt first, and they made me turn around and checked my arms for anything. Then before I could put on the paper gown they asked if I had a wire in my bra. I really thanked myself for deciding to wear a bra without wiring because they might have made me take it off or destroyed a beautiful bra. Next, I had to remove

I never thought my life would really mean that much to other people, but it obviously means more than what I thought.

my pants so they could check my legs for any more scars, then they gave me my paper gown pants. I had to remove my shoes and they gave me hospital socks. Finally, I removed my headband. They put everything in a big brown paper bag they said I'd get back later.

My mom was sitting in the chair with tears in her eyes when I walked in. "Don't cry, because it's going to make me cry," I said as tears started to form in my eyes too.

She wiped her tears and said, "It just made me think of when I was at Our Lady of Peace."

I realized how painful it was for her. I wanted to change and get better so much so I wouldn't keep seeing my family hurt and worried about me. I saw this tweet once where someone said, "Do you ever realize that you are a lot more traumatized than you realize?" I keep that in my mind anytime something happens that brings up some kind of negative feelings or little flashbacks for me or my mom. We all have memories and trauma that haven't been dealt with, and I could tell this was one of those times.

Growing up, my mom found herself in situations that weren't the best, seeing things that a child shouldn't have to, and she had to grow up early. She has told me a lot of stories since I was too young to remember. My birth was a wake-up call to most in my family.

She was a freshman in college when she got pregnant, so she didn't really get a chance to live the college life. When she found out, she was first confused, then upset and shocked. She went to see a counselor that same day because she was already homesick, and this just made her want to go home to my nana. It's interesting because of all the people in her family, my nana was the last person she told.

My mom went home for Thanksgiving a month later and never went back, so she was only at college for four months. She's enrolled in school a couple of times since, but never finished because it was a lot to take care of me and not really get a lot of help. My mom had to take me with her to school sometimes because my nana wasn't always available. She found it hard to study while at home and sometimes she just couldn't focus on her work.

When I was younger my nana used to have seizures a lot. My uncle or pawpaw would be home when it happened, but my mom was always the one who took the initiative to take care of my nana. She would need to sleep after having one and my mom was not comfortable with anyone else watching me. My uncle has a learning disability and doesn't always pay attention to detail. My pawpaw, while he tries to be a good guy, stays in trouble with the law. For these reasons, my mom worked hard but hasn't finished college. She used to tell me I was a blessing because, had I not been born, she would have probably gone down a destructive path herself.

I think my birth helped out my nana because I had to stay with her a lot. She taught me, and in the process, she learned something too. My nana sometimes has trouble reading and when she would read books to me, if she came across a word she needed help with, I was able to help her. She also loved drawing and drew pictures of different things that I loved. We would draw together and decorate the house with our drawings. I never thought my life would really mean that much to other people, but it obviously means more than what I thought.

I sat on the bed and a guy came in and asked me if I wanted anything: to watch TV, a blanket, some food, something to drink. I decided on the blanket and TV. He brought me a thin-ish blanket and the TV remote and said I could watch anything on TV except for Adult Swim which, coincidentally, I always watched and wanted to watch then. I scrolled through the channels and found the live-action *Cinderella*, which kept my mind distracted.

My mom stepped out of the room when an assistant psychiatrist came in to ask me some questions.

"Hello, my name is Christine. I'm going to just be asking you some questions since you're having to wait such a long time. We only have one psychiatrist and we want to try to cut down on wait time."

"Oh, okay," I say. *Guess this means I'll be here for a while.*

She started off asking me the basic questions: how long I'd been depressed, if I took medicine and what kind, how my moods changed, if I've ever harmed myself. *Ugh, it's boring answering these questions, and very uncomfortable. Opening up, letting people in to know how I feel, what I think and go through. It's nerve-racking.*

After I answered her questions, she reassured me the psychiatrist would be in as soon as he could. I didn't really care as long as it wasn't too long. She got up and left the room. I was stuck in this foreign room, cold, bored, unsure of what was to come next. Another lady came in to tell me that it was going to be a long wait for the psychiatrist to come in and that there were two people ahead of me. She offered me food. "Once it's gone, it's gone, then all I'll have is turkey sandwiches," she said. I thought I should probably eat so I could focus on something else. "Can I have a turkey sandwich?" I asked. She said yes and came back later with a box with the sandwich, condiments, chips, and applesauce.

"I don't like touching other people's food, so can you take the wrapper off the sandwich for me?"

"Yeah." I opened the box and took off the plastic wrap, thinking about how it was probably for people's safety, again. I handed the wrapper to her.

"Thank you. You know it's just so weird, I just don't like touching other people's food."

"Yeah. I understand," I said. We had a little chuckle together, which is just the natural response some people have at the end of a conversation, then she closed the door and I was left to my food and myself once again. *I'm going to be here forever,* I thought. I began to eat my food slower than I thought I ever had before. Even after adding mustard and mayo, the sandwich was a little dry and the turkey was shredded and mostly in the middle of the whole wheat bread. The soda was hot and gave me a weird memory of medicine. The pretzels and applesauce that came with it were good, at least.

I just wanted to sleep, but I thought I should probably stay awake for when my mom came back. I didn't know what time it was. I was freezing. I lay down. *Where is Mom? Why has she been gone so long?* My eyes were becoming heavy, the movie was becoming boring, and I drifted to sleep.

I woke when the assistant guy opened my door. "Hey, because of the wait time with the psychiatrist, we are having a video call with a psychiatrist to make things go faster."

My brain was really foggy and I thought, *I don't really care.* I'd just been woken up and I was hot now compared to the cold temperature from earlier. Why is it that when you sleep your body gets warmer and you end up waking up really hot?

He turned off the TV and turned on the lights, which were way too bright—you could see everything that was wrong in that light. I sat up as he dragged in the travel TV: a beige computer monitor on a silver stick with wheels on the bottom. There was a tiny basket hanging on the stick with a little sign that said *Travel Psychiatrist.* The background on the sign looked like a forest in the fall, with a brown and orange color scheme. The thing looked like the character Karen from *SpongeBob.*

The guy pulled the Karen thing in the room and closed the door. The guy on the screen was in his late thirties or early forties, with black hair and a black beard that was nice and trimmed, and a black sweater. He was sitting at some kind of desk, and I wondered how he'd gotten this set up. Where was this guy? What time was it there? Questions kept forming in my mind.

"So, this is going to be like he is really here but on a screen, all right?"

"All right." I just agreed. It wasn't the weirdest thing; it was as if I was doing an over the phone evaluation.

"Hi, I'm Dr. Beckley. You're Persia, right?" I could see myself on the screen in a little box in the lower right-hand corner. *God, I look a hot mess,* I thought.

Having natural hair that shapes itself when you're sleeping is irritating. *I don't care. They should let me go home.* I leaned on my right elbow and kept the cover on me, feeling uncomfortable in the gown.

"Correct," I said, making sure I kept eye contact. Even if we were talking through a monitor, I should still seem like I was paying attention and being respectful. In the end, he was only trying to help.

"All right, so I know you're probably tired of answering the same questions, but I'm just trying to get an accurate clue on how to help." Internally sighing, I nodded my head. "So, what brings you here today?"

I explained how my routine check-up had led to this. Sometimes I talked quietly, and the microphone on the machine was at the end of the bed. He'd ask me to repeat myself and I'd have to talk louder. I was sure everyone could hear me because the walls were thin. *Great,* I thought.

He wrote down what I said and I waited, observing myself in the camera. I have beautiful hair but it was dry, brittle, unkempt, damaged. I began to put my hand in my hair, feeling the unwashed, product-filled, stiff dead cells. I used my hands to pick it out with my fingers so it wouldn't look so bunched up and oddly shaped. This made an echoing sound in my head and I felt my heart pumping because I believed everyone could hear it as I picked my hair out.

Wow. I always look a mess, but this honestly feels like a personal low. I know I just woke up, but still. My body looks so gross on camera. Just makes me realize how much space is being taken up. Ugh. Sometimes I disgust myself so bad I feel the physical urge to throw up. I could've told him that. But why should I? It's something I can change. In all honesty it doesn't even matter. I'm complaining for no reason.

I looked down at the sign hanging from the monitor. I looked at the white text and traced those letters out with my big toe under the cover, keeping my mind focused, calming myself down.

"Tell me how your mood has been lately?"

How has my mood been? I don't even know. I feel like every day is a week and every week is a month. What is up with time? My emotions are always changing so quickly. The more depressed I've become, the more I realize that I don't understand it.

"It's been okay, I guess," I said. "I sometimes think I'm having a bad day or am in a bad mood, but I realize nothing has really happened, so I try to see it like I'm not in a bad mood. School makes me feel weird, but other than that, it's not like there is something happening to make me feel bad or anything." *Except me.*

He wrote down whatever analysis he had. When I was first going to therapy a year ago, my mom told me, "It's much better when you're a child than when you're an adult. They at least try to help you. But when you're an adult, they just sit there, listen to your problems, write them down, and tell you what they think. There's no real human emotion." I wonder if that's true. Maybe therapists just have a bad rep.

"Do you get easily angered or irritated?" he asked.

I chuckled to myself. "I get easily irritated. I wouldn't call it being easily angered because I can usually calm down or change my emotion to something else pretty quickly." I tried to look at the screen while answering his questions, but I kept looking down to see how I looked. Looking at him in a monitor felt very awkward, but I wanted to make it seem like the answers I was giving were true. Were they? When he was writing and no one was talking, it was so quiet that I felt like everyone could hear my thoughts like in "The Tell-Tale Heart." I glanced at the assistant guy who'd been sitting in the chair and wondered what he was thinking. He had to be listening to me, judging me. He was just looking down.

"Have you had a change in your lifestyle patterns? Like a change of appetite, eating too much or too little?" I shook my head no. "Getting too much or not enough sleep?" No again. "Has your performance in school changed lately?"

"I think so, a little," I mumbled.

"What was that?" He asked me to repeat myself. I sighed deeply and cleared my throat.

"I think it has slightly," I said, louder, getting even more anxious that I had to talk at this volume. I knew for a fact that everyone could probably hear me. "I think it's only because I'm a senior and I want to graduate, so I think it's a normal behavioral change."

"So, tell me how long you have been struggling with depression and anxiety? Is that correct?"

"Yes, I have anxiety as well." He nods his head for me to continue. "I believe it started or developed when I was in fifth grade maybe. I felt as though this girl was trying to steal my best friend, so I basically felt lonely. Then when seventh grade hit, I started to dislike everyone around me—my friends, the teachers, the students—and I think it started to either develop then or it got more noticeable. I was about thirteen then."

"So, you were basically suffering quietly."

Suffering? I wouldn't really call it that. Okay, I hate myself, which makes my depression worse, makes me feel lonely and isolated, like I can't trust anyone, like all my

friends are out to get me or going to leave; but I wouldn't call that suffering. Maybe that's my anxiety. So, what's my depression? I can't even tell anymore.

"Do you know anyone who has tried or committed suicide?" he asked.

I recalled last year when I hadn't talked to a friend of mine for a while. I thought maybe she had tried to kill herself or was severely ill. Then, when she came back around, she told me and our group of friends that she had tried to. I didn't know how to react. It didn't happen, so that was good. I got to be alone with her one day and we were talking about it, and she told me how she didn't want to. It was just that feeling where you believe that you have no more options, no one to turn to, that your situation won't get better, and your head is telling you, *Either keep getting hurt going through this, or end it all.* I know that feeling.

"Yes, I know two friends who tried to." It made me feel wrong for talking about other people's situations. It's not my place.

"How would you describe your anxiety?"

Having both anxiety and severe depression is torturous. The way it makes you feel like your brain is slowly disintegrating is gross. It makes life so much harder. Even solving or dealing with simple things is impossible.

"Well, I like to say that it's not that bad, but I have social anxiety. I don't have anxiety attacks or anything but sometimes it's up and my hands get shaky and my voice trembles."

He continued to write and turn pages. I noticed that his sleeves were pushed up and he had tattoos. *Oh, so I have a cool psychiatrist, then.* Tattoos mean he's artistic, creative, meaningful, maybe.

I looked down at the little black reflected round lens that gave off a hint of blue. I thought about how a camera is put together, how complicated it is to the average person who doesn't know how it's built, and I wanted to take it apart. I looked back up at me in that tiny little box on the screen.

"So, are you taking the following medicines: Prozac, fluoxetine, a daily multivitamin, Estarylla?" He asks, knocking me out of my thoughts.

I nod my head. "Yes."

"And you were taking ten milligrams of the Prozac and asked for an up in your dosage?"

"Yes. I started taking it a year ago. And then one time I ran out of my medicine and didn't tell my mom, so I didn't get a refill for a few days. Then I forgot to take it, and it just kept happening, so I stopped taking it."

"Was it working when you were taking it?"

"Well, I was taking it in the summertime and nothing was happening, so I couldn't really tell if it was working or not."

"Then you decided to start taking it again?"

"Yes, because I felt like I was getting more depressed, and I felt like I needed to start taking it again. But it didn't feel like it was helping really, so I decided after a while to ask my doctor to up my dosage."

"Then you stopped taking it about a week or two ago?"

"Yes, because one day I read that the medicine could cause dizziness and drowsiness and that night I went to bed after taking it and I woke up in the middle of the night really dizzy, so I stopped taking it."

"People who take Prozac don't tend to have the symptom of dizziness, so it could have been caused

She's my anchor for when I don't feel well or am confused and don't know what to do or who to turn to.

by something else. I suggest you start taking it again and if it happens again then tell your doctor about it and we can see if we can get you on something else."

"Okay."

"Okay, so I'm going to talk with your mom and then we'll go over what the best plan for you is and then you'll be good to go. Okay?"

"Okay."

"Do you have any questions before I go?"

I think and shake my head. "Nope." I never have questions.

"Okay, then, it was nice meeting you."

"Nice meeting you, too." The assistant guy opened the door and took Karen out of the room with a soft smile. He nodded on his way out and I did the same. Just another weird politeness thing.

I was stuck in the cold, colorless room, alone once again. I knew it was never good for me to be stuck in my head. I started to overthink, over-evaluate, to slip into a depression episode. I fought it, though. I knew that I couldn't slip into an episode with the possibility that someone could walk in. I was in a psychiatric evaluation center, and I was trying not to show that I was depressed. I was alone for a while with thoughts just roaming around in my head. I curled up on the bed, waiting, thinking, waiting, thinking—just repetition, and not a good one.

My mom came back to the room. She's my anchor for when I don't feel well or am confused and don't know what to do or who to turn to. I know she'll always be there for me and I'm thankful to have that, especially knowing that others aren't lucky enough to have that.

She came in and sat down in the chair as I looked at her. "Where have you been, bro?" I asked her.

"Well, I went out to talk with the psych lady, then I went to get my phone to call my friend Sarah. She was trying to calm me down since I was upset. Then by the time I started to feel better I came back inside and you were sleeping. They told me how they were going to do a video call with a psychiatrist. Then after they were done, he talked to me."

"Ugh, so what are they going to do now?" I asked, tired of being there. It felt like being in a casino: no sense of time, no clocks, no windows. The TV gave me few clues because movies keep playing, so no thirty-minute time marks like with shows.

"I guess they're going to figure out a plan for you and then I guess you get released." The door opened and we both turned our heads to see the staff guy who'd been helping me all night. He had the brown bag with my clothes in it and told us that the psychiatrist believed I was no harm to myself and that I was fit to go home.

I let out an internal breath that I hadn't known I was holding. I took the bag, went into the bathroom, and changed back into my regular clothes. Relieved to be back in my comfortable clothes, I put the gown and socks back in the bag and fluffed out my fro so it didn't look messy. I walked out of the bathroom and went up to the desk to give them the bag. I later found out that my mom had gotten a little paper showing why I had gone there, who had seen me, how I had a

follow up appointment with a pediatric psychiatrist, and that I was diagnosed with a new illness.

"Is everything you need out of here?" a lady asked me. I nodded and she threw the bag away. "All right, you're all set. Have a good night."

I was excited to get out of there. "You too," we replied.

I followed my mom as she led the way out. I felt a wave of relief wash over me when I finally got outside and saw the dark night sky and the quiet, mostly empty streets. I smelled the air and just felt comforted to not be in that place.

"Hey, what time is it?" I asked my mom as we walked around to the front of the hospital.

"Just past midnight." *Wow.* I was shocked. Even though it had only been a few hours, those few hours changed me.

After my evaluation, I started to focus on my mental health more, making sure to take care of myself, focusing on getting better. I started taking my medicine again, and it was working, even though I couldn't feel much changing. But I still wasn't where I wanted to be. A big part of it was loneliness. I knew I wasn't alone, but my brain still thought otherwise. I would occasionally take time to think about the people around me and how they felt lonely too. You find comfort when you notice that other people around you are going through the same thing. It's just a common human emotion. Knowing they are just as stressed and confused about what's next helps you realize that it's normal and nothing to be ashamed of.

School was the biggest problem for me. I was stressed and had breakdowns. It ruined my mood

thinking about it, but I had to go through it, so I needed to find a way to just push through. Thankfully, I had classes and peers that would help my day go faster and give me something to look forward to every day. The stress of what's next after high school, what I want to do in life, how I am going to achieve my goals? It's too much. I had to realize that my main goal was getting better.

Ever since the outbreak of COVID-19 happened and we've been in quarantine, I don't have mental breakdowns like before. I've just been staying home, learning more about myself, trying new hobbies, and I've really been able to take time for myself. I cherish this time. Sure, I wasn't able to go on our senior trip, and there was no prom, and we couldn't graduate like normal, but that just means no extra money spent. Will I miss it in the future? Maybe, but right now,

I don't care. Surprisingly, I've been doing really well, except for occasional anxiety from school. Since I wanted to focus on my mental health and not stress myself out too much, I would neglect the work that stressed me out and then get stressed out because I hadn't done the work I needed to graduate. What goes around comes around, right? What matters is how you handle it. I handled it poorly at first, by shutting down and not doing my work, but then I realized I really need to graduate, not just for me, but also for my family. When I thought about how they've helped me through school for all these years, I pushed through, did what I needed to, and graduated. It made my family so proud, especially my mom, who knew how hard and stressful it had been for me.

The only part of not graduating like normal that I will miss is not being able to have my family see me walk across the stage. It is what it is. We can't control it. My nana is at high risk for COVID-19 and hasn't been able to spend time with us lately, which is sad. We reach out to her more, and we talk just about every day, checking up on her and ordering the things she needs so she doesn't have to risk going outside. She got to see me in my cap and gown, though, and was so proud that I finally graduated.

My mom and I have been taking this quarantine well, except that having to work from home as a customer service center specialist, dealing with disrespectful and annoying people on the phone every day is taking a toll on her. But thankfully, being here means I can help calm her down and ease her mind, making sure she's okay. I'm so glad I can relax now for a while, figure myself out some more, and start the next chapter in my life. It feels so great that I pushed through and made it, that my depression is so much better, and that I've been changing as a person and growing up. I've been really proud of myself for doing what's good for me. That's always important, self-care. I don't take it for granted that I'm able to be in a good place during this pandemic. I know it's not a good time for those who are struggling. I hope it gets better for them. It will pass, like everything does.

NAUDIA
M. GREEN

I AM THE DANCER
I WANTED TO BE

It was a fondu, coupé, tendu, coupé, tendu, ball change, relevé, coupé, passé, and balance combination with left hand at the barre, starting with preparation in second, feet fifth position.

Classical ballet is like math: there is a right way to do everything. A lot of dancers start off their studies with classical ballet because they are often told it is the foundation of all dance and teaches techniques and mechanics that are universal throughout any form of dance. Most of my years of instruction were a contemporary amalgamation of ballet, jazz, and modern, all of whose movements and vernaculars stray away from Eurocentric dance and bring in elements of dances originating from Africa and African American culture. I only took three years of classical ballet, so when I encounter that dance form it's usually much more advanced than anything I've ever experienced.

The contemporary ballet company Complexions, founded by two dancers from the Alvin Ailey Company, had come to Louisville to give a master class and hold mock auditions for young dance students from the Louisville Ballet, Louisville Dance Alliance, and the group I danced with, ArtsReach, which offers female students professional-grade dance classes in the ballroom in the Chestnut Street YMCA. It would be a practice audition where the instructors would tell us what most professional auditions would expect of us.

The other girls in the room were around my age. They were all slimmer and towered over me. Clusters of dancers were scattered at the barres that stretched across the room, chatting as they stretched. It seemed like most of them knew each other. All of them were wearing ballet shoes and some form of leotard and tights. Some wore pink tights and black leotards, while others wore black tights and flashy leg warmers, or maybe even a tan leotard and tights. All of us from ArtsReach wore sweats and stood barefoot. Compared to the other dancers who spend six days a week in the dance studio compared to our one day a week, I knew we had no chance of impressing anyone.

The instructors, one male and the other female, were at most seven years older than me. It was so surreal seeing "the ideal dancer" in real life: long legs, slender frame, short torso, and long neck. I was mesmerized by the difference between me and them.

Not too much older than me, the male instructor was even from Louisville and had reached heights and accomplishments that I could only dream of. They were bubbly and energetic as they encouraged us to stretch before the first barre exercise.

I glanced around me, making eye contact with the girls from the other groups. Their eyes were trembling anxiously and I couldn't help but chuckle, thinking, *They'll be fine. It's us ArtsReach dancers who should be worried. Do we belong here?* Yet I wouldn't let myself be intimidated. I posted myself at the front barre so I could see the two instructors' feet while the other girls from ArtsReach lingered in the back. It was clear to me that this "audition" would be difficult.

I didn't spend the Saturday mornings of my childhood watching cartoons. I spent them in unoccupied school buildings and vacant church classrooms used as makeshift dance studios. I've been dancing since I was two years old and, even back that far, I can remember having a knack for performing. My parents spent hundreds of dollars paying for costumes, classes, and practice shoes because I loved dance. I loved performing. There was something about the familiar feeling of ice cold floor tiles shifting under my feet as we performed various dance showcases and concerts, about the beaming, piercing spotlights, and the horizon filled with people as I looked off the stage. I've never felt more at home. No matter how reserved I may be, I love being on stage.

To this day, hearing The Jackson Five's "Up On the House" or Kool Moe Dee's "Wild Wild West" entices me to softly pace through the choreography no matter where I am. My body still remembers these dances that I learned years ago as a member of a dance troupe called the La'Nita Rocknettes. I remember the choreography from tap dances that my parents don't even remember seeing. I remember tripping over loose tap shoes and stepping on untied ballet shoe strings, the missteps that could cause the teacher to make us start practice over and throw her shoes at our feet, and the hectic moments backstage when mothers would hover over their daughters and put bright red lipstick on both our cheeks and lips. I remember the times when we walked off stage as the curtains lowered and saw the faces of the teachers and Mrs. Neil (the founder of the La'Nita Rocknettes) congratulating us for doing a good job, but also telling us how we could have done better.

I wasn't exactly the outgoing type when it came to dancing with the Rocknettes. Other girls were much more talented and invested than I was, some spending at least four days a week dancing with Mrs. Neil and performing at various venues. I never danced alone; I've always been a part of a group. I was more of a filler who only stood out to my parents. This isn't to say that I couldn't dance, but if I were picked for a solo, it would be the teacher's intuition, not because I asked. My name was never plastered on the programs, nor did I get to dance at special venues for the company. I was good enough to be a face in the blur of twenty or so girls. I don't feel bitter or resentful. I just understood where I stood in comparison to others.

In middle school, we would go to the Louisville Ballet and Kentucky Center for the Arts to watch classical ballet dancers who stood tall as they glided across the stage practicing their leaps and bounds. They faced us with a calm and elegant expression, but underneath that, you could see the concentration in their eyes. I would lean back in the velvet-lined theater seats and tightly close my eyes, wishing to be like them, but I knew that I couldn't be. I could never reach the same leaping heights as them, not only because I was shorter, but also because I was bigger. I'm by no means the ideal dancer. I stand at around five feet tall, with short, stubby legs, and board-flat feet. I don't have the 5'5", slender frame with high arched feet. I've always been far from this perfection, and I'm okay with that. There is no use in trying to fix the things that can't be fixed. They're already meant to be. Since I've been dancing for as long as I have, I can understand when choreographers have to make stylistic choices to ensure that the dance will look good. After all, dancing isn't only about being able to do the movement, it's also about how you look in comparison to everyone else. Compared to other dancers I would stick out like a sore thumb because of how I made dances look. I was either too close to the floor or not close enough to the ceiling. Regardless, I was still a dancer, and I was proud of what I could do. I took every opportunity to show anybody who thought they could doubt me what I was made of.

I went to a performing arts middle school where I was a dance major. I wanted to be a dancer, so I thought this must be the only way. Every day we wore black leotards, pink tights, and ballet shoes. In my dance classes prior to middle school, if you had been trying your hardest and it had looked similar enough, differences in dancing styles had been acceptable. In this space, though, the goal was for everyone to look as uniform as possible. The amount of precision was the most jarring thing. I had to start over and build a foundation that had never existed. I had to become

better, even if that meant losing weight, even if that meant sweating to death during second period. My three years of middle school were spent focusing on technique for classical ballet, modern, and jazz with a few master classes in hip hop, classical ballet, and flamenco. The main focus was classical ballet, though, and it was my first encounter with how rigorous it could truly be.

Most dancers who seriously study spend five or six days in the studio for at least five hours at a time, constantly moving and perfecting technique, conditioning, and practicing muscle memory so they can learn dances by being *told* about them instead of seeing them. In my experience dance teachers didn't necessarily dance. They told us what to do and showed us with their hands. Like, when an instructor says the combination begins in fourth position

parallel, a dancer should automatically know to turn their toes out, heels facing front, with their weight evenly distributed between both legs.

In the Rocknettes, the majority of my time in a dance studio was spent learning choreography with a basic technique for warm ups, the names of movements sprinkled throughout the class, and how to properly execute them. But in middle school, we practiced technique solely. Barre combinations, across the floor combinations, and center combinations were used to drill technique. We would often do leap combinations across the floor and plie combinations at the barre or in the center of the dance floor. It wasn't until a month and a half before a performance that

our teacher would choreograph a dance. At this time, we would dance twice a day. The first dance period would be used for technique and the second would be used to learn and practice the dance.

After middle school some of the other girls in my dance class wanted to go to YPAS, Louisville's performing arts high school. But I couldn't dream of that no matter how tightly I closed my eyes at night. I wasn't meant to be the type of dancer they wanted no matter how many classes I took, at least not in this lifetime. The path I had been on contained limited stylistic choices as a dancer. Everyone was supposed to look the same; twelve people were to move as one, and I knew that wasn't going to be me. Unless you're twins, in dance you can't look exactly like another person. No two dancers are alike. I would have to eat, breathe, and sleep technique, and all I really wanted to do was dance. I no longer dreamed of becoming a professional dancer. I didn't have the dedication. I just wanted to dance and not follow anyone else's lead. So after middle school, I stopped dancing and engaged in new artistic endeavors.

But dance still came up every once in a while. I would find myself dancing for plays and after-school projects. When the Central High School theater department said they'd be producing a show called *Fame Jr.*, I got a little excited. The first person I talked to about the play was my father. He always loved it when I did musicals. One weekend we were at his old apartment just chilling on the couch, talking about our week, and flipping through channels trying to find something to watch.

"Yeah, Central is doing *Fame Jr.*," I told him.

"You mean *Fame* from the '80s? I remember that show!" he said. "I didn't know it had been made into a musical for kids. Should we watch the movies?"

I shrugged my shoulders. I had jumped at the chance to do another musical without really knowing what it was about. We watched the movie from the '80s and another that came out in the early 2000s. The stories are about the relationships and friendships between the students at a performing arts high school in New York. *Fame* follows these students from freshman to senior year as they deal with various struggles, some mundane, others unique. Illiteracy, substance abuse, heartbreak, and rejection are some of the themes. But the diverse characters all have the same dream: they want to be famous. They want their name in shining lights no matter what it takes. They

don't realize they're competing against each other, but when they finally do, they have to learn how to compete fairly.

In *Fame,* I played a character with a dream of becoming a dancer. Before coming to the performing arts high school, Tyra was a contemporary dancer with various influences that included classical ballet. But she had never been faced with a professional atmosphere prior to her entry into the performing arts high school. She just wanted to be part of something, even if she didn't fit in.

There was a time when, like Tyra, I wanted to be immortalized, to live forever underneath the shining lights. I strove most of my life to make this dream come true. I had been on my way to compete with hundreds of people for the same thing until Tyra and I went two separate paths. We both wanted to dance, but Tyra wanted to do it for the rest of her life while I didn't. I became tired of the leotards and ballet shoes. I gave up. But *Fame* gave me the experience of what I had missed out on by deciding to stop being a dance student in high school. I didn't regret my decision, and I still wasn't too keen on being a dancer again, but Mrs. White, who directed me in *Fame*, persuaded me to join the ArtsReach dance program. I think I joined because I felt an obligation. When someone asks me to do something with excitement and dedication in their voice I can't say no. I want to be the dream they see. So, in junior year, I started dancing hip-hop and contemporary modern with ArtsReach.

We were in our Thursday afternoon modern dance class when Mrs. White told us to gather around her as she began to speak. We gathered in the center of the ballroom floor as we waited for the rest of the conversation to take place. "The week after next,

practice will be on Wednesday because Complexions will be holding a master class for us and the students in the hip hop class." Murmurs from the others indicated a pique in interest.

"I love Complexions. The last time they were here it was cool to see them perform," one of the girls said. A lot of the others nodded along with her.

"On our usual practice day, we will be going to see them perform at the Brown Theatre. Lastly, they'll be holding a mock audition at the Louisville Ballet, and I want you guys to go and represent ArtsReach the best you can."

The master class would be a simple class where they would teach a bit of technique and possibly some choreography. It wasn't supposed to be as much of a learning experience as it was just pure fun.

On Wednesday afternoon the next week, I walked from Central High School to the Chestnut Street YMCA, where ArtsReach had their classes in the ballroom. Our hip hop and modern class were combined for the master class that day, and I wandered through the clusters of dancers looking for a place to put my backpack, sharing a few glances with the other dancers, who seemed to be excited. I lingered around the edges of the classroom, waiting for our instructor from Complexions to walk into the room.

He was about 5'2", pretty much at eye level with all of us. When he came in he said, "At Complexions we want to ensure that dance is for *everyone*, no matter how different you are. It doesn't matter your size, gender, or sexual orientation. If you love to dance, you deserve to participate." He continued to repeat this throughout the night, and he motioned to us that *we* were "everyone." Half of the time we were up in the air doing leaps, while the other half we spent "falling and catching" ourselves in a tendu combination. "I could see the excitement in your face. Anything I did, you did it with 120%. When you're as short as we are, it's fun being tall, it's fun to fly. In Complexions none of us look alike, one dance is done sixteen different ways." He said this to me at the end of practice and as I went home it stuck in my head. There are plenty of moments in my life where I've felt completely discouraged, but it was all in my head. People could tell me how good of a dancer I was, but I compared myself to other dancers and hated myself for differences that even I couldn't change.

But a professional's opinion means a lot. Not only was he a dancer with Complexions, but he had also danced with Alvin Ailey. *At this mock audition I'll give my 120% per usual*, I told myself.

I tend to be very pessimistic in every situation because I want to be extremely excited when something good happens. But I'm always happy to dance, especially in a real studio with tall vertical mirrors that don't dare have a fingerprint on them and ice-cold ballet barres that slide back and forth across black Marley floors without a scuff on them.

At the mock audition, I knew what types of exercises were coming, yet I wasn't nervous. I realized that I hadn't done classical ballet in years, but I also knew that all I had to do was dance with effort and everything would be fine. At the end of the day, it was just a mock audition for young dancers. This was just for the experience, for fun. We had been told by our teacher to experience all types of dance because the bigger one's body of experience, the better you look in the long run, both physically and mentally. The more dance forms you experience, the more open you are when you put them to use doing choreography.

The first combination they asked us to perform was a fondu, coupé, tendu, coupé, tendu, ball change, relevé, coupé, passé, and balance combination, left hand at the barre starting with preparation in second, feet fifth position.

I understood what they asked for. Fondu: to melt. Coupé: to cut. Passé: to pass. Tendu: tighten or stretch. I was no longer used to ballet, and the complexity of the combination took me by surprise. Once the music started my foot followed one step behind the dancers from Louisville Ballet and Louisville Dance Alliance. *Of course,* I thought. The instructors glided around the classroom, watching our feet and posture with a professional's intensity, and when they got to my barre they gave off a sympathetic smile and

We needed to regroup to understand what exactly had just happened.

quickly turned their eyes away from me. The lag that I was experiencing was embarrassing, to say the least.

"We want to see your flexibility and your ability to show us the difference between pure ballet technique and contemporary dance," the instructor said. I shrugged off the embarrassment of the barre exercises. *Don't let them see you fail,* I told myself. In my mind, I had done it to the best of my ability and I was content. I wanted to do better, but this wasn't the time or the place to get stressed.

I could see that the other girls from ArtsReach were struggling too. It was difficult to keep up when you had never experienced something like this, but we continued to make it work.

After the exercises we pulled ourselves to the back of the room and huddled in a circle. We needed to regroup to understand what exactly had just happened.

"I know I can dance, but this isn't what we do," one of us said. The other girls began voicing their opinions and we were all on the same page. "I can't believe Mrs. White would embarrass us like this. Is this what she means by 'experience'?"

Did she want us to experience shame and defeat with a sprinkle of pitying looks and words from other dancers? All the girls had low spirits, even the ones who said they didn't care.

We shimmied our shoulders to the beat, clapped our hands, and bobbed our heads: we were going to have fun our last time around.

"We'll be all right," I told them. "It's almost over, and we have nothing to prove." I understand how they felt, but I couldn't see Mrs. White wanting to embarrass us—she had just wanted us to experience something different, and the outcome had been less than ideal. I don't think anyone had expected things to be like this. We all had felt like the master class and mock audition would be similar, but we had been sorely mistaken. However, I know Mrs. White only wanted the best for us as dancers, and part of that was dancing outside of our comfort zone. Even after the audition she expressed how proud she was of us for taking the chance to experience something so different.

To this day I have a deep appreciation for Mrs. White as both an instructor and human being. She was the one who got me back into dance and provided me with multiple opportunities to expand and explore as a dancer. Whenever she has dance projects or dance performances, I am one of the first people she thinks of. I am glad to have met her, no matter what happened in this one experience.

"Star Dust," was the piece they chose to teach us. This David Bowie tribute choreographed by Dwight Rhoden was a line dance focused on footwork and core engagement. They taught the piece with speed and urgency, and I could feel the tension in the

room as people stared intensely at every flick, tap, chasse, and turn of the dancers, but I relaxed a bit. I knew I couldn't get any more embarrassed than I already was.

We were all split into three groups. Two groups would stand to the side while the other would perform as the two instructors stood in front of the class watching their movements. Each group went a total of three times before they called out a final group by the individual numbers on their chests. Every once in a while, they would rush to their roster to take notes. There were a total of eight people in my group, and three of us were from ArtsReach.

We were told to groove to the introduction of the song. I could see the people around me break into improvised duets with their friends, so we decided to do the same. We shimmied our shoulders to the beat, clapped our hands, and bobbed our heads: we were going to have fun our last time around. I have always been a quick learner. A few walk-throughs of a dance and I usually can get the gist and the quality of it. Then, after a few run-throughs of the dance full out, I can then grasp it in its entirety. I've developed this over time. All of the dance companies or dance groups that I've ever worked with choreographed dances quickly so we could have more time to practice the full dance multiple times and make changes as necessary.

Some dancers put movement to sound because you can't think about dancing while dancing. You ask yourself how the movement would sound instead of thinking of what it actually looks like. A slight click of the teeth to represent a flick of the foot or a snap of the fingers in the music has helped me learn a lot of dances that I can still remember.

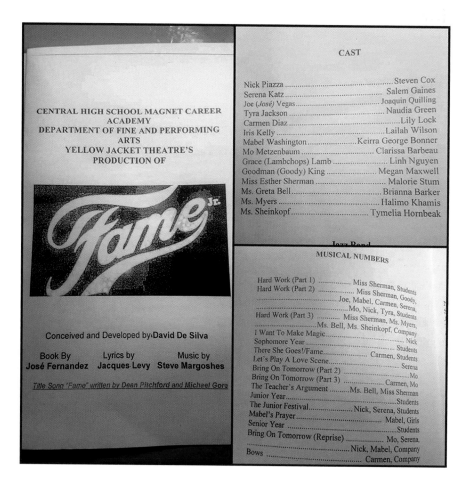

CENTRAL HIGH SCHOOL MAGNET CAREER
ACADEMY
DEPARTMENT OF FINE AND PERFORMING
ARTS
YELLOW JACKET THEATRE'S
PRODUCTION OF

Conceived and Developed by David De Silva

Book By José Fernandez   Lyrics by Jacques Levy   Music by Steve Margoshes

Title Song "Fame" written by Dean Pitchford and Michael Gore

CAST

Nick Piazza	Steven Cox
Serena Katz	Salem Gaines
Joe (José) Vegas	Joaquin Quilling
Tyra Jackson	Naudia Green
Carmen Diaz	Lily Lock
Iris Kelly	Lailah Wilson
Mabel Washington	Keirra George Bonner
Mo Metzenbaum	Clarissa Barbeau
Grace (Lambchops) Lamb	Linh Nguyen
Goodman (Goody) King	Megan Maxwell
Miss Esther Sherman	Malorie Stum
Ms. Greta Bell	Brianna Barker
Ms. Myers	Halimo Khamis
Ms. Sheinkopf	Tymelia Hornbeak

MUSICAL NUMBERS

Hard Work (Part 1)	Miss Sherman, Students
Hard Work (Part 2)	Miss Sherman, Goody,
	Joe, Mabel, Carmen, Serena,
	Mo, Nick, Tyra, Students
Hard Work (Part 3)	Miss Sherman, Ms. Myers,
	Ms. Bell, Ms. Sheinkopf, Company
I Want To Make Magic	Nick
Sophomore Year	Students
There She Goes!/Fame	Carmen, Students
Let's Play A Love Scene	Serena
Bring On Tomorrow (Part 2)	Mo
Bring On Tomorrow (Part 3)	Carmen, Mo
The Teacher's Argument	Ms. Bell, Miss Sherman
Junior Year	Students
The Junior Festival	Nick, Serena, Students
Mabel's Prayer	Mabel, Girls
Senior Year	Students
Bring On Tomorrow (Reprise)	Mo, Serena,
	Nick, Mabel, Company
Bows	Carmen, Company

Five numbers were called out before the instructor announced, "16, 19, and 20." The three of us from ArtsReach had been called out for one last dance. The instructors said we danced the piece the best out of all students. We may have fallen behind in technique, maybe we weren't as flexible as they would have liked, but when it came to actually dancing the choreography, we excelled. Among the eight, I'd reckon we were most confused as to why we were up there, but we quickly shrugged it off as the music played and we danced the final dance with whatever energy we had left in us.

At the end of the audition, we were sat down in the center for feedback by numbers. "16, 19, and 20. We are shocked by your ability to be uncomfortable and embarrassed and still do your best." I tightly closed my lips and chuckled under my breath. *Was that supposed to be a compliment?*

Throughout that whole entire day, we had been told, "If I were to do hip hop, I wouldn't do as great." I would retort with, "I'm a modern dancer and I used to dance classical ballet, so I'm not really good with hip hop either." With a few words the professionals in the room solidified everyone's thoughts: *They're not meant to be here.* Even though the looks on our faces pleaded for them to stop, they continued, "This is an experience to prepare you for the future. This should give you a signal about whether you should continue to strive to dance professionally or you shouldn't." Their words clung to our skin like molasses. I felt like I was being pulled under, and the other dancers in the room couldn't help but look back at us. We silently looked back and forth at each other, and in that silence, we knew it was time for us to leave. We grabbed what was left of our existence as dancers and left quickly while everyone else stayed behind trying to speak with the instructors. We exchanged a few glances and nods before everyone finally left.

In the vacant hallways of the Louisville Ballet, I waited for my mother to pick me up. I had been excited to dance in an actual studio with professionals, but by the end, the build-up of pitying looks and sighs and backhanded compliments almost drove me over the edge. I was disgusted by the pity they gave us.

I can't really put a finger on what makes me want to dance. It's something that just flows. Dance is an escape from the life I normally live. Real life is depressing and boring, it reeks of pencil shavings and the ticking of analog clocks. Performance is disembodiment from the rest of the world. When I dance, sing, or act, my brain goes static and my body, my lips move on autopilot. But everything comes to an end. There is no such thing as forever. In a world that is constantly changing, so do the minds of the people within it. I am different.

I spent more than a decade giving myself to art. I'll always remember the trips and falls, the sore calves, and the beautiful choreography that came during recitals, concerts, and showcases. All these moments are scrapbooked in my brain to recall at any moment. The songs are trips down memory lane that drive and move me through times of boredom and anxiety. I can have bathroom dance parties when I've gotten a little too anxious, or I can just think about some of the fun times as life gets harder. But dance will never disappear from my life. It just won't be my focus.

For the longest time I've walked a thin line with dance. I love to dance, but I also don't want to commit. With organized dance comes the need to be

conventional, like the dancer everyone wants me to be. But I'm not here to please others. The dancer that I want to be can change her mind any time and place in her life. So maybe I'll pick up a few things every now and then, but I have a focus, the place I want to be in five years, ten years, and twenty years that doesn't involve dance directly. But that doesn't stop me from enjoying a good K-pop cover dance.

I'll always be a dancer no matter what stage of life I'm in. As a child, I breathed dance. I could never get it off my brain. Every conversation I had somehow made its way back to dance. I would talk about the long Saturday morning practices where my age group would sit and wait for the babies to get done. We would lace up our tap shoes, walk into the classroom, and warm up with quick stretches. Sometimes the older dancers would drop in and watch as we practiced. Then Mrs. Neil would come in and glance over every dance before they were completed and finalized. She analyzed our movements and would often make abrupt changes in steps. Any misstep could result in a shoe being thrown at your feet, but it was usually funny. Her criticisms were always with reasons—there was never a "just because" or a "because I feel like it"—and would always benefit the dancers and the dance itself.

I enjoyed dancing the most when she was around, and a lot of that joy left when she passed. In that setting, I learned how to be an individual. Dancing with the Rocknettes made me unafraid to stand out. It made me unafraid to work harder and smarter. The ideals that dance has embedded in my mind are continuously in effect. Active recall, self-discipline, precision: they have all made me the person I am today. All the dancing I did wasn't enough to make me the dancer Complexions wanted. But I don't think I wanted to be that dancer. I'll come out stronger. Just wait and see.

ANIIA
D. CHERRY

STILL YOURSELF
BUT NOT THE SAME

Growing up, my father wasn't home much, but I never asked why. I missed simple things like him checking on us in our rooms or tucking us in at night. I missed that. But I always understood that he had a very important job helping millions of people that he didn't even know. Being the daughter of a Marine doesn't mean you're able to go where they go.

If I'd been able to take a peek through my mother's belly button in Germany, I would have seen all of the beautiful buildings there and could have listened to techno music, all while cuddling in my mom's amniotic sac. I did this for about a month before we moved to Louisville, Kentucky, where I was born.

A Marine's daughter is just a regular girl who may have traveled a little more and who has weird-looking swords hanging in her living room in places where regular people might have pictures of their families. If you walked downstairs at our house, you'd think it was just a regular old creepy basement: a room with a washer/dryer, a living room, a room with a couple of beds, etc. But there was another room with a lock on the door, and we had been told since we were little kids to only go inside with my dad or if it was an emergency. I'd only been in "the black room" a few times. In one corner there stood a green and gray army suit from when he served in the U.S. Army, and in the other corner he had his black Marine dress uniform with medals pinned on the front and a white hat on the table. The room was filled with nine or ten gun cases. One side had a bunch of pictures of my father in the army, the other side had cabinets and shelves filled with his most prized collection: boats! Big boats, little boats, ships, all types of boats. In the far back part of the room we kept our Christmas decorations, reindeers, and wreaths.

Being a Marine's daughter means that my father is extremely strict and old fashioned. As a child I didn't really understand why, but as I grew up, I learned how to cope and move around it. Obviously there were no boyfriends, staying out late at parties, or really even asking to go to a party at all. It also means that I've watched *Full Metal Jacket* at least a hundred times. My dad explains how true and realistic the movie is, but I still have no idea what is going on in the story.

Aniia's father

I don't know how many times my family was forced to pack their bags and move to a new town growing up. I don't remember how old I was, but I hadn't started elementary school yet when we took a trip to Alabama for our summer vacation and I was told that we might even move there. I didn't fully understand what this meant, but I was excited to see some change. I hated how boring Louisville was and I'd always beg my parents to take us on vacations.

"Oh please don't speak too soon!" my mother said. "There will be plenty of 'vacations.' So many that you may even become bored of them."

I didn't know what she meant by this but I soon figured it out as, almost every year, we packed our bags, left behind all the bonds we'd made, and moved on to make new ones. It was tiring.

I'm the daughter of a Marine, but somehow I'm still able to get attached to people, to build close bonds with them, and in the end I'm still hurt when I'm forced to leave. Over the years I've grown out of it some, and it's become easier for me to distance myself and have the same "I don't care" attitude that I learned from watching my father.

As I grew older and was enrolled in school, my parents decided that it wasn't okay to move us around as much as they did. My father would be doing most of the "living" and "moving" from place to place, while my mother and siblings and I would just vacation to these places. This meant that the only times throughout the year that we would see our father was whenever he came to visit or when we went to visit him during the summer break or Christmas break. But what seemed to be such a great idea at first wasn't really a great idea after all. It took a huge toll on all of us to be completely away from our dad for two years with my mother forced to raise her children on her own. Deep down, everyone was hurt.

Eventually my mother had enough. My dad had been living out of town for all of this time, and she was tired of sitting around all day every day, unable to work, without the man she married at home with her. Once, on a weekend when my father had come home, my parents sat my siblings and me down at the table. The conversation started with us sharing how we felt about each other and how much we all loved one another, then quickly changed to my parents saying that they would no longer be together. My mother's exact words were, "The six of us will no longer be living together." I felt confused. I didn't really understand what it meant at the time. I was barely entering the first grade, and I'd already lost the thing that was most precious to me: my family. They were all I knew. Looking back on my life, I realize now that this was the beginning of my acceptance of separation, of being okay with people walking out on me. Time after time, it became easier, and I wouldn't question the repetitive cycle in my life. It's something I've been used to since forever ago.

I vividly remember the custody hearing. I expected a lot more halls to turn down inside the courthouse, which was kind of small, not like the ones you'd see on TV. I can remember sitting in the long row of seats, like at church but much more uncomfortable, listening to lots of people and their different cases. When it was our turn, there wasn't really a question about who we wanted to live with. It was just a set thing that we'd be living with our mom, and that we would spend weekends and breaks from school at my dad's house.

Oddly, when my parents gained joint custody of my sister Angel and me, I was happy because it meant I was able to have an individual relationship with each of them. My father had moved back to Louisville to have joint custody. Every Friday after school, my sister and I would walk home since the school was literally around the corner. We didn't really have to pack up any clothes to go to my dad's because we usually had some left over from the previous times, and if not, he'd just buy us new ones. Almost every weekend was another adventure. My daddy always had something different for us to do, whether it was taking mini-trips to Lexington or just hanging out and going to the movies together.

Staying home with my mother was a little different, though. Ever since she'd become a stay at home mother, we were inseparable. I slept with my mom until I was nearly in the third grade. Every night I'd lie in the same position on my mother's bum and talk her to death. Going to school was a struggle most of the time because I couldn't stand being away from my mother for such a long time.

Throughout all the emotional, spiritual, and psychological effects of the divorce, she didn't have time to manifest and be to herself. Like a double-knotted string, she was confused about how to get out of her previous relationship, but she wanted so badly to be loved. It seemed to me that she had been doing fine on her own, but I guess she didn't think so, and after about two years of being divorced and single, my mother began mingling. I was eight years old when my mother introduced us to a new man. He was 6'6", buff, his head round and his face always freshly shaved. He wore baggy old clothing and any old sneakers he could find.

This man had a slight smirk to his face. It wasn't a normal smile, though. It was deception.

This man had a slight smirk to his face. It wasn't a normal smile, though. It was deception. The smile of a faker. The smile of a liar. The smile of a hurt human being. The smile of a broken soul. The type of smile a man puts on right before he lays his hands on your mother. The type of smile he puts on while whipping those same hands across her face repeatedly. The type of smile that gloats when hearing her children scream at the top of their lungs for someone, anyone, to help. It was the same smile he uses with her children after pretending like nothing ever happened. The same smile he has when he knows that the woman still won't leave him, that she will pack her clothes for the night and return bright and early the next morning. The same smile he shows her family when they see her black eye and he promises them that he will never do anything to hurt her again.

I copied that same smile for my professional pictures once. I woke up the morning after Easter that year, ready to finally get these pictures over with. I practiced my smile as we walked in. As I leaned against the white stool decorated with flowers, he stood next to me, breathing over my shoulder and forcing me to smile a very painful and insincere smile. He whispered to me the entire time, promising those same lies he'd promised my mother and our family:

"It's okay, everything's going to be just fine." He gently touched my face, pulling both sides of my mouth upward, positioning my face for a smile. When my face returned to a scowl, he would apply force like he did to my mother.

I'd get extremely scared and anxious when he came around. Being alone with him made me feel horrible inside. At times I would be so afraid that I'd burst into tears. I was always so overwhelmed with fear, and crying was my only release.

He made my siblings and me read the Bible several times a week. We took turns reading one verse apiece. He listened, then had us reflect on what we read, trying to make us understand it. I don't think *he* understood it. Sometimes when I had to read a verse to him alone, he tried so hard to be this comforting "dad" that it made me want to throw up inside.

He said that only he would be allowed to work and provide for the family, so that meant my mother was forced to be a stay at home mother, once again. The thought of her getting a job completely ate him up inside. He didn't like independence, especially not for women.

My mother is a powerful, Black female. A role model in my eyes. It hurt me to see her going through something like this. I consider myself the luckiest girl in the world to have a woman with such a beautiful spirit as my mother. Ever since I can remember, my mother has been someone I've looked up to. My hero wasn't Beyoncé or Michelle Obama like it was for most kids my age, it was my mother. In my eyes, my mother was way better than any of those women could ever be for me. Her devotion and ambition are inspiring. She's taught me to walk, talk, take care of myself, and to always be a strong independent

Black woman, and if she hadn't taught me to take such small steps, I wouldn't be able to take the bigger ones. But even with her guidance, I still struggled with the situation.

My school friends noticed that I wasn't the same person anymore. They'd always seen me as jolly and excited, but now I didn't ever want to do anything with them. I started to push away everyone I'd ever loved. I let myself totally fail in everything. I flushed all of my accomplishments down the toilet. I was involved in cheerleading and track, but I never gave my best effort anymore. All of my first and second place finishes turned into lasts fast. Everyone in my school life worked with me to get me back to where I was before.

Mr. Johnson was my teacher at Jacob Elementary School. He had the voice of a man who had lost his vocal cords, like he was struggling to talk. He was not only my first male teacher but most importantly he was my first Black male teacher. Mr. Johnson was such a bubbly, cheerful, spirit-lifting, and eagerly exciting person. He made sure to keep everyone smiling and happy. If you needed a laugh or any type of uplift, he was in no doubt the person to turn to. I always walked into his class extremely excited but being sure not to show it because of how shy I was.

"Is that Aniia Cherry?" he'd yell all the way down the halls, stretching out each syllable every time he saw me. I felt like he was my best friend in teacher form. He'd give me words of wisdom and made sure I knew exactly who I was and what I was capable of. He would never let me believe that I was anything less. Mr. Johnson wanted me to be the best me

possible and that's why I was so close to him. He was the father that I was missing at the moment. He had filled that piece of my heart.

No matter how things were going at home with my mother's situation I chose not to make it my own. If I did, I knew I would be so geeked up that I wouldn't allow myself any time to think of my own problems or celebrate any of my Hollywood endings, and I wouldn't prosper. This is when I began my journey in band. At first I had trouble picturing myself in the band. But it was love at first blow into my clarinet, and I ran home with my permission slip, yelling at my mother to sign it.

My instructor was Mr. Demby, who also taught our choir class. He was super tall and had big feet, so he wore these really long dress shoes. His voice was extremely deep. He also had a shaking problem. He could barely even hold an instrument without looking as if he was going to drop it. But he never did. He could play every instrument beautifully, but his favorite was the saxophone. He had patience with us, despite the fact that we sounded horrible and could barely play, and he taught us all how to properly blow into our horns and the correct positioning for our fingers. Holding down your pointer and middle finger along with your thumb in the back would come out like a sharp screech instead of an E sharp if you didn't remember to moisten the reed with saliva before you played.

I had way too much stage fright to attend most of the concerts that year. When I did perform, I'd pack up my instrument so quickly afterwards that no one had the time to congratulate me or even look my way before I'd sped back to the band room, heart pumping out of my chest.

In seventh grade we had five concerts planned, plus pep rallies and assemblies. That year I played in one of the major concert trios with two of my best friends. All of us had the same extreme fears of playing in front of other students, our parents, teachers, and the public. But I practiced for about a month and stayed after school for one-on-one sessions with my instructor, Ms. Arndt. She taught me to sing each piece to myself in my head and visualize what we were playing instead of thinking about how many people were in the crowd staring at me. "Tap your foot and sing the song inside your head." Jin-gle-bells. D-D-D. Tap-Tap-Tap. For the first time, I wasn't worried about seeing my mom in the bleachers. I focused my attention strictly on the sheet music and, in the end, it played out well.

I didn't just use this technique in the band room or at concerts; whenever I was in class and my anxiety started to bother me, I practiced in my head. I practiced my concert sheet music, I practiced my solo pieces, I practiced upcoming test pieces, I just practiced. Eventually, after having played in front of so many different crowds and performing solos, I was able to grow out of my shyness. I became more outspoken and confident. However, when I was at home, it was a totally different thing—I had a hard time learning a technique that would help me shut out the constant screaming and yelling.

It was 2:00 a.m. and there I was, heart racing, sweat dripping, awoken to the sound of my mother crying. She was screaming at the top of her lungs, begging for mercy. I threw my covers onto the floor and hopped into one of my older sisters' beds. My sisters hadn't been woken by the loud piercing cries of my mother yet, which was unbelievable. I shook them both, without caring if I disturbed their dreams. When they woke, they immediately grew aware of what I was so shaken up about. Tears poured from each of our eyes, and without waiting for my sisters to figure out what we were going to do about it, I ran out and into the next room.

"Let her go!" I screamed at the top of my lungs as I swung through the door. "Leave her alone! You're hurting her!"

I don't know what made me speak these words. I was always so afraid of him that I never even thought about speaking anything out of the ordinary around him. He seemed to have so much power. It was like he held my entire life in his hands. Maybe I was just fed up with his bullshit, or maybe it was the fact that it was almost three in the morning and I had to be up for school in a couple hours. Either way, he didn't stop. He launched his hand back even farther and punched her right in the face.

I'd never actually seen him hit my mother, only the scabs and scars after the fact. My eyes stopped blinking and filled with tears. My mouth locked into an O shape. My feet couldn't take another step forward. I was in complete shock. My mom begged and pleaded for us to go back to our rooms. I ran over to meet my mother, rubbing her arms and using my own shirt to wipe off the blood. I wanted her to be okay, I wanted her to feel my comfort. I wanted all the pain and baggage she was carrying to just leave. I wanted to be the one carrying it instead. But it never worked like that.

"Mind your business. I'm showing yo momma something! Go on back in there!" he yelled.

And just as I was going to respond, my sister pulled me by my shirt and dragged me into our room.

"Are you out of your damn mind, Aniia?"

I couldn't answer the question because I didn't understand why she was asking me instead of him; he was the one who was out of his mind.

"I'm 'bout to call the police," she said. My sister was crying and shaking so hard that I wondered if she could even hold the phone. Her voice was quivering, and I could feel the heartbrokenness within every word she spoke. She was pacing around the room in circles, struggling to catch her breath as she sobbed on the phone with the police. They promised her everything would be all right and that they'd make sure of it.

My oldest sister went to the kitchen and grabbed a broom, a can, and a knife. When she came back, she gave my other sister the broom, handed me the can, held the knife herself, and told us to use them as we please. She said that at any given moment if we felt the need to do so, DO IT! We didn't really need to be informed of what the "doing it" was. What else would we be doing to a 6'6" man who had been beating the hell out of our mother for years now? It wasn't my first rodeo. Things like this happened a lot around there.

It was only a few minutes before we heard police sirens. I'm not sure if he heard them or if he even knew the sirens were for him. We sat our weapons on the bed and stood by the front door. We couldn't wait for the police officer to knock on the door and have us explain to him why he should take him to jail.

Hard knocks banged against the door, and we barely let him knock before we quickly swung the door open. There stood a really tall, white man, not too big or too skinny. He had a little hair on his head and a slight beard growing in. He seemed a little bored and uninterested by the way his eyes wandered when we spoke. "Hey ladies, I need you guys to calm down and tell me who he is, okay?" We each nodded as we turned in the direction of their room.

"HE HIT OUR MOMMA!"

"HE'S IN THE ROOM," my oldest sister yelled as she pointed in the direction of the room he was in.

"Are you gonna tell him we called you? Can you just go take him with you?" I whispered to the officer loud enough for him to hear, but quiet enough for the abuser not to. I didn't want my sisters to hear me either. I wasn't just afraid of being his next victim, but even more scared to show I was scared, especially in front of the strongest people I knew.

Then the abuser was there, standing over top of us all.

"How can I help you, officer?" he walked up to the door as if he were trying to intimidate the man.

"The police were called by someone who said they heard a bunch of yelling and screaming from this residence. Just wondering if everything was okay?" My heart warmed. The police were finally on our side. He had lied for us! I'd never in life had an officer lie for me, but in that moment, I loved every bit of it. I felt powerful. Undefeated.

"Everything is fine, officer." the abuser said. "It's almost 5:00 a.m. We've been sleeping and it's pretty obvious that you're interrupting us. I don't know why anyone would say something like that. I mean, do you hear anything?" At this point the officer had let himself in. He was standing in our living room with his flashlight in his hand. He seemed to be observing the abuser, while the abuser, on the other hand, had

been showing off his acting skills, rubbing his eyes and yawning as if he'd really been sleeping.

I needed my mom. I needed her to come running out, showing all of the red scarring and ugly marks he'd drawn all over her body. I wanted so badly for the officer to say, "Yes." To lie just once more for us. I knew that if only he'd taken a few more steps out of the living room he'd be able to see all the mess in the hall, or if he'd gone to the bedroom where everything had happened, he'd see all the mess my mother had created while trying to protect herself. But instead the officer replied with, "No, it's all right. Sorry to bother you all. You all get back to sleep and have a good day!"

My heart dropped. The police officer stared into my eyes. He knew something was wrong, but he didn't care. He ignored the blood stains on my shirt. The tears in my eyes obviously meant nothing to him. His eyes kept looking into mine as he walked through our living room and exited through the door.

Maybe it was fear that I'd noticed in him before. Maybe he'd shared the same fear that we had and it had taken over. But he betrayed us all. I never wanted to call the police again. I questioned if the police were even good for anything. We called the police on him many times, but they never took him. Our word never seemed to matter. They never wanted to investigate, never believed us, never asked any questions. Each time, we were left hopeless. My mom was left in a trap. The hope she had of leaving narrowed each time the police turned their backs on her.

As the officer hurried away, the abuser slowly turned and looked at each of us. I wanted to look at my sisters for some type of reassurance, but I knew better. My neck wouldn't even allow me to look over. My head wouldn't dare move.

"If y'all ever do some shit like that again, you'll see exactly what I can do. We gon' see if y'all ever pick up another phone again in your life."

I was terrified at this point. I'd never been threatened. Even today I think back and still don't know if I've ever heard anything more powerful said to me. I walked back to my room and cried for mercy, begging to be returned to what life was like before all of this.

I will never allow a man to treat me like this. I made sure I told myself this all the time.

Why did she stay? I spat at her weakness. When I asked my mom, she gave me the same answer. "There was nowhere else to go." But this wasn't true.

"I want my daddy!!!!" I'd scream as loud as I could so that someone could hear me, so someone, anyone, could bring him back to us.

But my dad didn't know what was happening, and, looking back, a lot of anger and confusion ran through my mind. Anger that I was never able to tell my father about what was going on. Confusion about why he wasn't able to see any clues in the way we acted around him. Every Friday after school, I was so excited to go with my dad when my sister and I went

to meet him at the corner of our street. He would sit parked in the car waiting for us, and as we walked up, he always made sure to greet us by getting out of the car and welcoming us with a huge hug and a kiss on the forehead. We lived only about ten minutes away from him, so our car rides usually didn't involve talking much, and when we did he usually asked about school or how we were doing. I was afraid to tell him. I thought I was protecting my father, but from what? Maybe I was afraid of what the abuser would do to him if he tried to handle the situation on his own.

Going to my father's house was everything I could ask for, though. It took my mind off of everything and allowed me to be a child again. We had Friday night movie nights where we'd go get snacks from Kroger, get a Redbox movie, and pop it in at home and cuddle up together. Dad never cared what movie it was. He'd watch anything we wanted to watch. And for all of our breaks off from school, he made sure we had the time of our lives by taking us on road trips and vacations to the beach. Anytime something went wrong or I needed something, he was the one I called on. I felt loved when I was with him, and in that time I needed every bit of it. I knew my parents loved each other and I wanted nothing more than for them to be together again. I thought of what it had been like as a child, about the times when everything had been okay, when I didn't have to beg for him because he was already there.

I had been all packed up for at least a week, but of course I continued looking through all of my bags to make sure I hadn't left anything out. The day before

Aniia and her sister with their father

we set off for Disney World I ran down the steps into the kitchen.

"Hey Ms. Loveable!" This was the nickname my father had given me as a baby. He told me that ever since the day I was born, I had been a loving child, always wanting to cuddle and hug, never wanting to fight. "Very self-centered," he'd say. "But loving."

"Hey Daddy! What you doing? Are we leaving yet?" I was always excited to travel.

"Almost. Just give me a few more hours to get everything situated and we'll leave. How about you watch that mummy movie with your sister? By the time it's over we should be all ready to go." I had probably watched that movie a hundred times and I still got excited each time. I fell asleep during the movie, and my father decided not to wake me. When I woke up, I could hear the cars and trucks flying by.

As we came alongside a semi-truck, my sister and I would make eye contact and positioned our arms to make "choo-choo" motions and give them the sign to blow the horn. We learned this from our parents; growing up always on the road, we would become bored of ourselves and find new ways to make excitement spark on our trip. We stayed in our RV as we usually did, decked out with a bed for each of us.

"Wakey wakey, my beautiful girl!" I could feel my father's cold hands shaking me on the shoulder. He had kept the air up way too high the night before and we were all freezing our butts off. The smell of Johnsonville sausage links filled the room and I stretched into the morning light. "Ms. Loveable, come eat your breakfast before it gets too cold." After bathing and putting on my favorite Minnie Mouse polka-dotted dress, we headed on our way to Disney World.

As we came along the next exit, I could see the sign to the side of the road that read *Hollywood Studios*. "We're here, girls!" my dad yelled out with more excitement than we had.

He was always the more excited one when we went on trips. He loved exploring and being in new environments.

Although my father was a rather serious and unrelenting person, he never failed to show how much he cared for me. I was his rock and he was mine. I had always been "daddy's little princess." I would've gotten it stamped on my skin if I could have. As we walked through the park I found myself only focusing on my father. As he held my hand, it felt as if somehow our veins were connected. I loved how warm and rich it felt. I felt protected, like no one could take me from him. I no longer had to worry about being

woken out of my sleep to loud siren-like screams or fists pounding against anything or anyone in sight. I was carefree in that moment. I had finally escaped *him*. Finally escaped that smile.

My father has always been my rock, and although he's always done everything he could for my siblings and me, the only thing I'd wished for, more than any gift or any trip, was to have a bond built on communication and listening. But even though we spent a lot of time together, and even though he made everything feel better when I was with him, I needed him to search deeper. I needed my dad to ask more questions, to make me talk more specifically about my at-home life. I'm not saying that he didn't do all that he could, but there could have been a lot more talking and opening up to each other. I just feel as if a lot of things were covered up with gifts. I was young,

so being given a gift took my mind off of things, but they were things I really should've been talking about. I wanted nothing more than for my dad to be my go-to person, and looking back, that might have prevented a lot of things that were going on with my mother and siblings and me.

As a child, I didn't want to talk much, and my parents never pushed me to talk about the stuff that was going on, which only made it worse as I grew up, and only makes it harder for me to talk to people now. I needed someone to vent to. I needed someone to take us out of the environment we were in, and not just for a three-day weekend. If I could go back and do it all over again, I would open up to my father and let it all out, because holding it in only makes it worse. No matter how many years go by, holding it in still hurts. Even after the "pain is gone" the pain is still there. The hurt and the guilt and the "what if's" are always there.

It was one of the last times we'd called the police. My mother had specifically told us to stop calling them, but the abuser had been beating on my mother for over twenty minutes. The screams for him to stop made my body quiver. My mother had no phone because he wouldn't let her have one because, "The only people you need to talk to are right here in the house with you." We weren't allowed to have phones either, and the house phone no longer worked for calling out but was instead transformed into a weapon. We'd decided the only thing we could do was walk to the closest store, which was about a five-minute walk.

When we got there and asked to use their phone, they wouldn't let us. The store clerk told us that the store up the street had a payphone outside of it. It was another five-minute walk to the parking lot of the next store. There was a group of men standing around the payphone sharing a beer, each taking a turn chugging it. The drunk men stared like they were preying on all of us.

"Excuse me, may we use the phone please?"

"Oh yeah, baby, my bad. I'm sorry, here you go." He talked like a drunk, using way too many words. He handed my oldest sister the phone. I could smell liquor and beer mixed on his breath.

As my sister grabbed the phone, she quickly dialed 911. We moved closer to one another as she gestured for us to do so. She handed my other sister the phone and told her to tell them exactly what had happened. She held on to both of our hands, making sure that we were all right next to each other.

The operator asked us all the same questions we'd been asked a million times before:

What's your emergency?

Can you tell me exactly what happened?

Where are you ladies right now?

Is he near you?

Can he hear us talking?

Is your mother breathing?

That was the scariest question of them all.

We answered in a rush, hoping to hurry and get to the point. So many questions, only for them to probably do nothing about it.

When we got back to the house, all we could do was wait. He was still in the other room beating her, she was still crying, the door was still locked. We sat on the couch next to each other. I began to focus on the green recliner we had in the living room.

I've shown enough compassion to those who've hurt me; now it's time to show compassion for myself.

It was my great grandpa's. He'd given it to my mother before he passed away. No one ever really sat in it. I used to imagine he was sitting there. I caught myself thinking about when he had been alive. Not much would be different if he were still alive, but I liked the idea of thinking it would be.

When the police finally arrived it felt like we'd been waiting for days. My mother's face had been used as a boxing bag. She had so many bruises and a black eye; she was bleeding. And all I could think was this being the time. The time we'd all been waiting for. For us to finally have him locked up and us finally being able to move on with our lives. Just us!

Once the abuser found out that it was the police at the door, he threatened us and told us not to step foot near the door. He was going to answer it. He put on his fake act for the police officer. I could tell that when the officer looked farther through the door at me and my siblings he understood something was wrong. Yet he had no intentions of fixing it. Again.

My sisters and I had called the police so many times, expecting something to change, but it never did. They'd show up, stare at the abuser for a few seconds and suggest, "There isn't a problem here." How do you abuse someone, in front of their children, have visible evidence, and not go to jail?

My mother stayed with this man for about two more years and finally one day he got drunk, wrecked his van into a pole, and was arrested for DUI and reckless endangerment. We finally moved out while he was in jail. My mother didn't tell him we were leaving; we just left and never returned.

In some ways, the abuse never stopped, though. It roamed through my head at night when I was sleeping. Something as simple as a cabinet slamming still makes me think of all the times the cabinets would slam in that house as my mom was pushed around. For most people that sound means nothing more than getting some food, but for me it means a lot more. It means aggression. It means someone's in trouble, it calls out, "Help!" Hearing someone slam anything has always been traumatic for my ears. It sets me back, stops me from being the best me that I can be. I know how much I've grown, but I can also see the ways that I'm still stuck in the exact same place I was years ago.

As I look back, I now understand what I was missing. I needed someone to pay attention. I needed someone to ask questions. I needed to feel wanted and to feel as if I was worth something more than what I was being shown. Every day I continue replacing the voice that tells me, "I need to be good to everyone," with another that says, "I am good to those who are good to me, and I protect myself from those who are not." I've shown enough compassion to those who've hurt me; now it's time to show compassion for myself.

I've been thinking about an undeniable truth that the victims of abuse share: when it's all over, people expect you to come out "victorious." No one tells you how hard it is to not feel like you're still trapped. No one tells you about the endless nights that you stay up because you can't sleep or the nights you get shaken up out of your sleep from the nightmares of PTSD.

No one tells you how to overcome those things. It's something I had to go through for myself. Although you will come out victorious, you will not come out the same as you were when you entered. You will be broken but hopeful, healed but scarred. You are still yourself—but you are not the same, and that is okay.

I don't think I've ever heard my mother speak out about being a victim, and she's not the type to hide, so for her to push the situation to the side and just forget about it and move on says a lot. She hasn't let that part of her story define who she is, nor did she let it affect who she wanted to become. I like to think that her heart is about the size of her entire body, because she's such a caring person. My mother is my best friend and my ride or die.

She was always worrying and putting others first. She still works hard every day of the week, working overtime in order to provide us with a better life, but she now has a bit more time for herself, and she utilizes it well. She spends her free time journaling, cooking up vegan meals, or watching documentaries about Black people, educating herself and those around her about African heritage and what it is we stand for. Her love for her own culture and traditions is to die for. You'd be lucky if you could get my mom to go out and party or anything of that sort. "Hanging out" for her means reading up on the latest news reports or shopping and ordering "unnecessary" clothes.

Her best friends are her husband and children. Sometimes when I come home from school, I'll hang out in my mom's room. Most of the time, she's already gone off to work, and when I enter her room, she's laid my favorite blanket out on her bed for me to use whenever I am ready to watch Netflix. She makes it seem like a sweet thing for me, when in reality it's

because she doesn't want to come home to a messy unmade bed. She has an old-fashioned DVD player that she refuses to get rid of because "it still works," and I usually find the same DVD case there with these drawings of African kings and queens with red, black, green, and yellow and all types of abstract art. *African Hebrew Israelites of Jerusalem. Hebrew or the So-Called Negro? The Ancient Black Hebrews.* She has so many of those things that I have stopped keeping up with what episode she is on. Each one is almost three hours long. She comes straight home and throws in a DVD that she has probably watched over a million times already.

Every year for as long as I can remember, my mom has had this tradition where she goes to her children's schools or jobs to bring them gifts on their birthdays. For some reason, she didn't do that on my

Aniia's mother and stepfather

birthday this past year. I was upset all day at school. Every time I heard a teacher's classroom phone ring, I hoped they were calling me down to the office to pick up my gifts. Even though I'd received a gift from my best friend, my mother's gift was the only one that mattered at the moment.

I walked into my mother's room that day after school, and flicked on the light. I had no intentions of doing anything or going anywhere. I was getting older now and didn't really enjoy celebrating with big groups of friends anymore. Before I could throw my book bag onto her floor and kick my shoes across the room, I was attacked.

"SURPRISE!"

There stood my entire heart in one room. My mother.

She stood there with balloons in one hand and a cake in the other. The cake was my favorite flavor, of course: strawberry. It was decorated with yellow and purple icing and had a picture of myself that I hated, but for some reason my mom thought it was the most beautiful one I'd ever taken.

She'd planned a surprise birthday party for me. The room was filled with balloons of all sizes and my favorite colors, on the bed lay the same amount of cards I received each year, one from my mom, one from my stepfather, and a card from each of my siblings. They'd each written lengthy notes about the reasons that they loved having me as a sister. Each card made me cry harder than the last. Later she made me a personal spa with a warm bubble bath and a pampered massage. I loved it all.

My mother has always been my best friend and my go-to, whether it's sitting in the kitchen annoying her while she cooks my favorite meal, or just simply being able to talk to her and have deep conversations about things I could never tell anyone else, She's the most generous person I know. She gives us every-thing, without ever wanting anything in return.

My parents have always been my everything. As for my father, our relationship is growing daily. He's still an army-strong man at heart, but his warm hugs and kisses always allow me to feel safe and secure whenever I'm with him. I know he loves me as much as I love him and wants nothing but the best for me.

I wouldn't say my life has been rough, and I wouldn't project this image that my parents didn't give me the most incredible chances and make my life everything I could dream of. Abuse wasn't a number one factor in my life; I didn't let it make me, and I surely didn't let it break me. What has helped the most is being intertwined with my siblings and our parents. My family has always meant the world to me; without them I am nothing. Having the people that I love most by my side as I face problems is what allows me to move on.

When I was younger I believed that every hardship was followed by a happy ending, that in the end you'd come out on top of the villain, and that life is this big "happily ever after." As I got older I realized that was a cliché. I realized that in order to get that happy ending, you have to strive for it and give it to yourself. You must believe that you are a precious human being and that you will always deserve better than what life throws your way and that you should be treated that way. I've had to be my own friend, and I've had to forgive myself. I'm still pushing for my happily ever after.

HALIMA

DAYS INSIDE OF DAYS

On September 11, 2012, I was in fifth grade. My teacher did what every other teacher did that day, which was show a video to the class. It's the first time I'd ever seen images of the two planes hitting the towers. I had no idea what the video was saying since I was still learning English, but it made me sick. I heard Muslim names, which made me uncomfortable. It felt like everyone in the classroom was looking at me, and for a minute I just wanted to disappear.

As soon as I got home I asked my mother, "What happened on September 11, 2001?" She told me how innocent people were killed that day. I was confused, and when I asked her why, she just looked at me and said she didn't know, but that they claimed to be Muslims even though it's *haram* to kill others. When I was growing up in Somalia, Al-Shabaab were doing the same thing, so I figured that the 9/11 attackers were no different from them. We know they were extremists, but the problem is that many non-Muslims label all Muslims the same. Even though I was not even alive in 2001, my life was written before I was born. 9/11 changed everything for the Muslims

in America. When I arrived in America in 2011 the hate was too real and too strong.

A few years ago, the holiday of Eid al-Adha was on September 11, which made it worse because people thought we were celebrating the 9/11 attacks. A boy in my class made a joke saying that my family was a part of 9/11. It makes me sick how someone can think a group of people are all the same just because that's what the media shows. It's sad that some people believe what they see and what they hear rather than finding the answer themselves. I sometimes do not know what people hate most about me, the color of my skin or my religion. It hurt me that someone compared me to the ones who killed people.

After school I sometimes take a walk with my grandmother around our neighborhood. One afternoon in 2017, we were walking and a red truck slowed down. He rolled his window down and he yelled out, "Fuck Muslims!" I didn't know how to react to this at all. I was just standing there lost in my thoughts. My grandmother looked at me and said, "What did he say?"

I was really confused. "I don't know," I told her, and I started laughing. It was my first time experiencing anything like that. I never thought that it would happen to me. I never thought I would worry about things like that here. America has given me a chance, but sometimes, when mosques are being attacked, or when many Americans don't want "others" to come into this country, I wonder what the real definition of an American is. I feel like I have to prove myself all the time for some reason. Even though I am an American citizen, I think that I am many Americans' definition of "The Other," and that's why I want to share my story: to inform them that I am human and that I have feelings too.

Remembering Somalia can be painful. I sometimes feel like my past is a shadow that follows me everywhere I go. So much happened in my childhood. Some things that I don't want to remember, and other things that make me laugh. Sometimes, from nowhere, I remember things from the past. They feel like dreams. Like witnessing my best friend die, the feeling I got when I heard my grandmother had been shot, or realizing that some people I used to see every day are now gone forever. Even though it was ten years ago, those feelings and memories will never go away. I sometimes tell myself that all the things I went through were just imagined. Yes, I do wish I could erase some of my memories; no child should know the feeling that their life can be taken away in a second. I used to ask myself why I had to go through all that, but the older I get, the more I understand. I might be seventeen, but I am thankful for all the pain that I endured because all the challenges that I am going to face are nothing compared to what I have already been through.

Growing up in Somalia, some days more than a hundred people would die in a terrorist attack, but no one talked about it. Not even the news. Mothers buried their children, and kids lost their parents. Every day I used to hear gunshots like it was the 4th of July. Sometimes I would go to sleep to the sounds at night and wake up to them in the morning. It got to the point where the sound of guns and bombs became our alarm. Everyone lost hope and was ready for their time to meet God. They didn't care about life. They had given up on the idea of living. Some thought that death was better than the life they had. It was as if their graves were already ready for them. It got to the point where people stopped showing emotions when someone passed away. Every day there was a funeral. The front of my house became a graveyard for the whole neighborhood. They say that children have the right to be free and protected here in America, but what about those whom I have known? What about those who never got the chance to grow up? What about those I loved whose memories are still part of me?

The Somali government was fighting Al-Shabaab, and we lived in between the two groups. When they got into fights we were affected heavily. One of the battles that scared me the most happened in the middle of the night. Al-Shabaab wanted to attack the government at night because they thought it was easier than the daytime, but the government fired back. I woke up to a sound that was so terrifying. It was a life or death situation, but I knew the drill. It had become instinct. My family gathered together and asked if everyone was there. After that, we slowly walked to the mosque because its walls were strong enough that

bullets wouldn't get through. The night made it harder to see since it was dark outside, and walking to the mosque meant that you could get hit anytime. We got there and waited hours for it to be over. The kids my age went to sleep to run away from their reality. I could not even close my eyes.

I have always lied for my brother Abdiwahab, especially when we were kids. I guess it was because we were close. I wanted to play soccer with him and his friends, so I would listen to him and do what he told me to. One day, we were walking to dugsi—Islamic school—and he said that he didn't want to go. He'd already finished the Quran so he wanted to go play with his friends. He told me that he would be back before class was over. I told him okay. When class was over, I waited for him for a while then went home, hoping that he was going to be there. But he wasn't home.

My family asked where he was, and I lied and told them he went to play with his friend after class was over. As the day went by my family started to worry and asked me again, "Where is your brother?" and I lied again. Hours later we heard the familiar sounds. It was happening again, and this time I had no idea where my brother was. We got to the safe building that was made of bricks that were strong enough for bullets. We looked for him there. I thought it was all my fault and that I shouldn't have held the lie for that long. When it got silent again we looked for him. Hours later he came back home as if nothing had happened. When he got home we were relieved. The whole time he had been gone he had been with the Ethiopians, who were in Somalia to help stop the civil war. The sounds we had heard earlier were close

to where he had been. Even though I was mad at him, I was also mad at myself for lying to my family. I promised myself to not lie anymore, especially in serious situations. Over the years I have broken those promises. Sometimes it is better to lie because it's easier and the truth hurts.

Since it was getting dangerous in Mogadishu, my uncles gathered us together and said that if anyone wanted to move to Kahda, in the country, they could provide the ride. This was the first time I'd ever left Mogadishu. On the road, I looked out the window and all I saw were plantations, which were new to me. I thought about my life in Mogadishu and the good moments I'd had with my friends, like playing hide-and-seek and talking about who was better at things like cleaning. When I was with them, I felt like myself. I did not have to hide anything about myself from them since I knew them all my life. Even though we were living through a hard time, we were like any other group of girls. We would go watch the boys play soccer and make fun of them. After coming from dugsi, we would meet and play dress up, make toys from things we could find around us, and play my favorite game, ladu, which is a dice game.

My cousin Sadia was one of the girls I used to play with. She and her mother used to visit our area. Since most people that lived by us were family, she stayed over sometimes. Sadia was the type of person who liked doing her own thing. She was so spoiled since she was an only child. Even though I couldn't relate to her, I liked how she got what she wanted. She did not care what others thought of her at all. She was the type of person anyone could talk to easily, and I liked that about her. When we first met, we became friends quickly. I liked showing her around when she came over.

When we got to the countryside in Kahda, we had to start all over again. My grandmother and the other women gathered around to help each other build their homes out of sticks and things we could find around us. The houses were oval shaped with roofs made of layers of clothes so the wind didn't get in. We had to wait for water and food, which came once a day. We had to share supplies with everyone. Each family had the same amount of provisions so it could be fair. After staying there for months we decided to move to Kenya because it was safer. We woke up early in the morning and got ready. We said goodbye to our friends and family again. We were some of the lucky ones. My family was able to leave Somalia to find a better life.

The car ride to Kenya was really long and tiring. We made a couple of stops to eat, sleep, or use the restroom, and we stayed a couple days at my aunt's house to rest. To keep us from wandering off, my grandmother would tell us scary stories about a lion who eats people. Even though I did not believe it, I still didn't want to go missing. It's kind of funny to me to this day because years later, my little sister still believed it was true.

None of this was new to me because my grandmother used to tell us stories every night before going to sleep. She told me stories that she used to hear as a child. My favorite was a scary story about Dhegdheer, or "long ear," in which a woman with a long ear can hear everything and eats kids. At the end, the kids put hot oil in her long ear. I liked hearing it before going to sleep.

Mogadishu market similar to what Halima remembers from her childhood

Another story my grandma used to tell me was about Queen Arawelo, the first feminist who fought for women's rights. She was very smart and knew what she wanted. She hanged men by their genitals to reverse the gender roles in Somalia. Sometimes being called "Arawelo" by a man was considered very offensive, but my grandmother taught me that it was a powerful name, and if I was being called that, I was doing something right. My grandmother taught me that if you really want something you should go and get it.

At night I slept next to my grandmother, and she told me stories of how brave my mother was. I hadn't seen my mom since I was three years old. She called us from the U.S. when she could and sent the money she made. I didn't remember my mother,

but my grandmother's stories made me admire her. To me she sounded so brave and strong. She was always speaking out against stuff, and when there was fighting in the area, my mom took a gun and protected herself. She would fight with and would make food for the guys. She was always the type of person to do things that females normally wouldn't do. She was open-minded. My mother had wanted to go to America for as long as she could remember, but when she told others, they would tell her to stop dreaming about it. Even though everyone doubted her, she didn't let it stop her.

My mom had an arranged marriage when she was just fourteen years old. After her father passed away, they lived on another man's land and ate the food he provided. He was very good to them, so when he proposed that my mother marry his son, the family could not reject the offer. When she was pregnant with me, there was a drought in Somalia, so they were having a hard time getting food. She was always hungry and didn't have enough to eat. My mom tried many ways to get out of the life she was in. After she had me and my two brothers, she left with my dad to cross the Sahara Desert so they could end up somewhere in Europe to provide for the family. They came back because she was pregnant with my little sister. Finally, the U.N. offered her the opportunity to come to America and, in 2008, she arrived and started working there.

That's when my grandmother replaced my mother and gave us the same love and affection. For as long as I can remember, I called her Hooyo, which means "Mom." My grandmother is a role model and much more to me. She always made sure everyone ate before her. There were times when she didn't have much left for herself, but she took what she had and gave it to someone who needed it more than she did—even people she had never met a day in her life. She's one of the strongest people I know. Her mother passed away when she was just a child, and she married when she was a teenager. Her first two kids passed away. One of them was shot while she was holding him and a bullet went through her. Even though she went through a lot of dark times she didn't let that change her. She was always smiling and happy that she got to see another day. My grandmother is a very religious person that doesn't miss any prayer. She tells me every day that the reason she does all the things she does is because she has God. You don't find many people like her.

Sadia didn't live by us but would visit us all the time. Once, her mother was visiting Ethiopia and she stayed with us. We played all day together. I think it was a Friday since we didn't have dugsi that day. It was a quiet day until around the afternoon when bullets started flying. They were everywhere and we didn't know what directions they were coming from. It was sudden, and everyone was just running for their lives. When everyone was in the mosque, the sound of shooting started to get closer and louder, so we ran to the tall tower where my grandfather used to stay.

My whole family made it there safely, which made me happy. We were just waiting for the fight to stop so we could go home. It lasted about four hours that day. It was one of the longest ones that I remember. Sadia and I were both close to the door, and she told me that she had forgotten her shoes. I told her that it was okay, that it was not the right moment to be worrying about shoes. She told me that her mother had gotten the shoes for her before she left and asked me to go with her to get them. I told her, "I will ask Hooyo if we can go." My grandmother said no, but when I got back Sadia was not there. I looked out the door and saw her holding her shoes. The next thing I saw was her falling down with a loud sound. As I watched her fall, I rushed out the door. Someone stopped me and held me down and tears were falling from my eyes. Just like that, she was gone.

Once after a stop on our way to Kenya, we got in the car and the driver told us to stay quiet and not move. This was nothing new to me. I was used to it. I asked my aunt what was going on, and she said that we were going to cross Al-Shabaab territory. I got scared and

All you could see were their eyes and nothing else. Everyone was nervous and didn't move.

stayed as quiet as I could. I thought to myself, *Not them again.* I was used to the idea of our lives being on the line, but my heart was racing so fast that I felt like I could hear it. After a while the car stopped. They were checking every car that passed through the street. I heard a man talking to the driver, asking questions about where we were going, then telling him to pull over. All the men in our car had to get out and were questioned. The Al-Shabaab men had their faces covered up. All you could see were their eyes and nothing else. Everyone was nervous and didn't move. The men pointed guns at the driver and ordered him to get out too and asked him more questions. After a while they opened the door to take a look at us. At that moment my heart dropped. Everyone avoided eye contact with them since we were scared that they were going to do something to us. They told the driver to get back in the car and finally let us go.

We were relieved when we got to the border of Kenya that night, but then they would not let us in. They said that they didn't know if we were working with Al-Shabaab or not. They questioned all of us and kept asking about them. We told them that we were running away from Al-Shabaab so we could be safe, but they didn't care about that at all. They had a Somali man working with them. He looked at me

and said that he knew me. He asked me, "Where are you all going? Don't lie to me." I told him what he wanted to hear, which was that we were going to the refugee camp. He looked at me with a serious look in his eyes. He thought that I had just lied to him and said that we had to pay them to let us in. We paid them, and after five hours they let us go. We got back in the car and thanked God.

The car ride was silent most of the time. We made a couple stops to eat and use the restroom. In the afternoon we got to a place called Dhagaxley (which means "rock"), which was the first refugee camp I had seen in my life. The environment was different. Everything felt strange, even the air. It was very hot. I could not understand how all of these people had left their homes and businesses behind so they could live in a place that looked like it was made of dirt. The injera we ate in the morning tasted very salty.

We could not stay there for a long time because my uncle was waiting for us at another camp. So, after resting, we took another ride to the refugee camp at Dadaab where my uncle had a place ready for us.

As we pulled up, I stopped to see the new house that was going to be my new home. I thought about all that we had gone through to get there. Dadaab was so hot that I would take my shoes off so I could feel the sand on my feet. It was one of the largest refugee camps in the world. Dadaab had refugees who had lived there since all the way back in early 1992, those who had escaped as soon as the Somali civil war started. This was surprising to me; I had had no idea that the war had been happening for that long. I saw people who had been born there and had known nothing but the refugee camp life. At Dadaab there were also people from Sudan, Ethiopia, and

People celebrating Eid on the beach in Mogadishu

other countries who ended up there because of things that were going on in their countries. It was my first time seeing different types of Africans. Everyone had a different reason for why they were there, but the stories sounded very similar: it was because of war, and they were all running away from something. All of them came and made that place home. We settled down, and after a while I got used to it.

When I lived in Dadaab, I was told a scary and weird story about our neighbors. They were Sudanese, I believe. They were really tall and had dark skin. They spoke a whole different language which I did not recognize. I was told that they killed people and ate them afterward. I wondered how in the world a person could do that. The next few days I walked over to see what they looked like. After I came from dugsi, I would

walk by their area. I watched them from far away. They were always laughing and playing. I was attracted to them because they were different and I wanted to know more about them. I went up to them while they were playing soccer and waited for the ball to come my way so I would have a reason to approach them. After watching them play for a few minutes they kicked the ball my way and waited for me to pass it back. I regretted how I had been afraid of them and wished that I could go back and approach them long before.

I had one of the best Eids that year because, for the first time, we didn't have to worry about violence. I woke up to the sound of adhan, the call to prayer. I hurried and put on my best dress. I got my henna done by my aunt Falis. She was really good at henna since she practiced on me and my sister all the time.

Dugsi (Islamic school) in Dadaab, much like the one Halima attended

We went to attend the Eid prayer. It was there where everyone checked out each other's clothes and saw all our friends. All us kids got money and gifts from adults after saying "Eid Mubarak." When we got home I helped prepare delicious dishes with my aunts. Friends and relatives were invited to feasts. The rest of the day I played with my friends. Eid was the time when I felt the happiest because I was with my family, and that meant everything to me. Eid was important to me because it had been part of me from the beginning of my life. This Eid was different because it was very peaceful. Peace was a word I knew but had no idea what it felt like until then.

About a month later I found out that we were moving again, this time to a refugee camp in Kenya called Kakuma. We had only two weeks to get ready. We had to leave our great-uncle behind too. It was sad because I was just getting to know him. We'd made Dadaab our new home but now we were moving.

They had about eighteen buses waiting for us the next week. We got into the number seven bus and we made stops to rest at night. I loved the long ride at night. We passed Nairobi one night. It was beautiful, and I told myself that one day I would come back to it. We drove all day until we got to Kakuma where they gave us a place to sleep and food to eat for the first day.

The block we lived in was called Block Y. The first few weeks it seemed unlivable. Kakuma was hotter than Dadaab. One night it rained so hard that water came through our tents. We started to build houses out of rocks and bricks and got used to living like this.

I started school. I had always wanted to go to school but this was the first time I had the chance to. I used to hang out with boys who went to school and they would tell me what they were learning. Sometimes I would sit by the door so I could hear what they were learning. When my elder brother started to take English I used to take his book at night. I always wanted to know more about everything and I was a good listener. I was really excited to attend school, but it didn't last long since we had to move to America.

Since my mother was in America she wanted to bring us there to live with her. We got interview after interview. We got checked to see if we had any diseases, and were asked questions about our mother, father, and everything in our family. After months of going back and forth, one day they told us that we had to get ready to move to America to live with my mom, whom I hadn't seen in six years.

I hadn't really known about death until Sadia was killed. It was then I realized the pain of grief. I had never felt it before. I think that us humans don't really care until it happens to us and we have to face reality. Realizing that you could be gone at any second was very scary.

I didn't want to go to her funeral. I blamed myself for everything because I was supposed to look after her that day since she was staying with us. When I saw the

My goodbyes were real goodbyes because I knew I might never see them again.

environment I was in and saw how easily life could be taken away, I made a wish and prayed to God. I prayed to God that I wanted to die in my sleep that night. I cried myself to sleep. I woke up the next day mad, wondering what I was doing still in the world.

I asked my grandmother, "Why did it have to be her?" She said, "We are all going to die one day, and when the day comes nothing can stop us." I started to question myself about God.

The day we left Kakuma to move to America, we got up early in the morning and got our belongings and said goodbye to our friends and neighbors. I was getting used to moving and saying goodbye to people. My goodbyes were real goodbyes because I knew I might never see them again.

My grandmother gathered the four of us together and told us to respect our mother. She said she was going to miss us. I couldn't imagine life without her. She was all that I knew. She was supposed to go with us since we were too young to travel by ourselves, but then they said we'd have to wait if she was coming, and that the processes could take a year or even longer. I didn't mind waiting. I just wanted her to come, but she said she didn't want us to stay because of her.

We took a car to a small airplane waiting to take us to Nairobi. Here we were in an airplane with people I didn't even know, with no parent or guardian with us. Just the four of us. I was excited at first because the idea of seeing my mother again after all these years was overwhelming, but leaving my family and friends behind was hard.

They had a bus waiting for us and took us to this place that looked like a hotel. We had to stay at that hotel until we were allowed to go to America. Those seven days were the longest seven days of my life. Even looking back now, it still feels like it was longer than seven days; it felt like it had days within its own days.

I will never forget the hunger and the cold I felt during this period of time. I never knew what it was like not having parents or someone to look out for me until it was just the four of us. Even though we had each other, we still felt lonely because we had no one else. The other kids our age had their moms and dads with them. The oldest among us was my brother who was only ten at the time. The youngest of us was my little sister who was only seven. People thought that we were going to America because we were being adopted or something. They felt bad for us even though they didn't know us. I did not like getting looked at that way. It made me feel small. I remember talking to this lady that was leaving for Canada. We were sitting under a shadow of a tree and she asked me where my mother was. I lied to her and told her she was sleeping. She looked at me and said, "I heard they got kids here without parents and I thought you were one of them." I acted surprised. She just kept going on about how she felt bad for them and how she wondered what happened to their parents. I couldn't tell her the truth because I didn't want her to pity me, to feel bad for us, like we were something to look down on.

At Kakuma everyone used to talk about how life was so much better in Nairobi. It was as if they had lied to me. The hotel was more of a jail to me than a hotel. We could not get out once we entered the hotel, couldn't go outside for anything at all. The hotel had two big doors as a gate. The only time it was open was when someone was coming in or leaving. The hotel had four floors and the bottom floor had a kitchen. The line was long and we had to wait to get our food. The other side was where the restroom was. I did not understand the staff because we did not speak the same language. It was hard asking for things that we needed.

We had to share a room with another family, this lady and her kids. My brother had the phone numbers of my uncles and aunts. He asked the lady for her phone and she talked to my grandma, who told the lady to look out for us since we had no one with us. She said okay, and we used her phone to stay connected with our family. My family trusted her because she acted differently when she talked to them. She was respectful and sounded kind. My family had never seen this woman in their lifetime, but because she was a mother, and had enough kids, and was Somali, my family trusted her. But that's how us Somalis are: we trust people easily. I guess they all expected her to do the right thing since she was a Muslim.

The next day she called my aunt Falis and told her that we needed food and that we were not getting enough. When she got the food she did not give any of it to us. She fed her kids first and ate the rest herself. She was getting meaner by the hour. When it was night, she would take our blankets. Growing up in Somalia it was always warm, so I had never felt

cold before. I wasn't prepared for it. Night time was cold and scary. It was as if time just stopped for hours. I could not sleep at all.

From that day on, whatever she told me to do, I did. She made me clean up after her kids. I had to clean the restroom after them. My siblings would not listen to her and would tell me not to listen to her either because she wasn't our mother. But she would give me back my blanket at night if I did what she told me, and I would give it to my little sister and brother. Just seeing them not cold made me happier and proud. So I started not to mind the work she told me to do, even though my siblings hated it.

Even though I don't remember her name or her face I can't forget what she made us go through. I woke up to hearing my name. "Halima." At first I thought it was my dream but then I slowly opened my eyes and saw her. I jumped up and she started yelling my name louder. The youngest of her kids was using the restroom and she wanted me to clean after him. I slowly walked over and thought to myself, "Why am I doing this?" But I did it. I wanted to go out and walk around, but she told me to stay and watch her kids. My siblings didn't listen to her and went out to play with other kids around our age. When they came back she would punish them. I wanted deep down to walk out just like them but I just didn't know how to say no. She could have treated me any way she wanted and I would still have listened to her. I didn't like that about myself.

And then it was Seven Days Eid. We couldn't celebrate Eid with our family and it made me sad. Aunt Falis was not there to do my henna. In Somalia, everyone went out to eat or to the beach on Eid but

I was stuck inside. Eid was usually the time when I felt the happiest since I was with my family, and that meant everything to me. Eid was part of me. But that morning I stayed in my bed. I didn't get dressed to go to morning prayer. There were no gifts of money or candy. I started wondering what others were doing and what fun I was going to miss out on. The whole day I looked at the window and just wanted to go home. I wanted to see my grandma and just hug her. I wanted to tell her how much I hated this place. I didn't care about America. I just wanted to go home to my uncles and aunts who loved us so much.

One night before we had left Kakuma, it was so hot in my room that I couldn't sleep. I decided to sleep outside. When I woke up the next day I couldn't move at all. My whole body hurt really badly. It was the worst pain I'd ever felt in my life. It felt as if my soul was being snatched from my body. When my family noticed it, they said that I would get better over time. I rested the whole day but it was getting worse. The next morning my uncle took me to the hospital. They said that I had been bitten by a scorpion. I was really scared and thought that maybe it was time for me to die. I remembered how I'd wanted to die after Sadia was killed, but now I didn't want to die anymore. I prayed.

When I woke up the next day my uncle Omar said he was going to take me to another expert, but this time I didn't want to go because I'd given up and accepted death. I told my uncle to let me go, that it was my time. My family refused and he took me. They gave me the medicine I needed, and the next day I woke up and felt better.

I had never before felt what it was like to be so close to death. I had felt ready. But part of me hadn't wanted to die. Not because I was scared, but because of the things that I would miss. I thanked God and understood that He could take my soul anytime He wanted. It had been a mistake for me to pray for death when Sadia died. Some people don't get the choice.

Our seven days at the hotel were over. We took a bus to the airport and had to wait for hours to get on the airplane. Since we were too young to travel and had no adult with us, they had a woman waiting for us to take us to our mother. Even though we didn't understand her at all because she was speaking Kiswahili and English, she seemed like she knew what she was doing. She looked like she had done this before. After a long time of waiting we finally got on the airplane. There were a lot of people on the airplane and they were going to different countries. The lady who stayed with us at the hotel was there too, but we only had to ride one airplane with her because she was going to a different state than we were. The whole trip, the lady that was at the airport stayed with us and looked after us. Every time we stopped I thought that we were in America.

The journey was long and tiring. We landed in Washington, D.C. and stopped at a hotel to sleep at night. It was a really cold winter night and we didn't have the proper clothes for that weather. I started to wish that someone had warned me that it was going to be colder than Kenya. When we got to the hotel it was warm. My siblings and I had to share two beds. They were big beds with white sheets and were better than most beds that I had slept on. I couldn't

understand how it was colder than Kenya but the room felt warmer. That woman who was traveling with us even stayed and slept in the room with us. We took long showers and changed into our new clothing. We were all so excited that we couldn't sleep that night. We looked out the hotel windows to see the beautiful view and the lights at night.

I couldn't believe that I was in America. Everyone I knew had always talked about how life was way better and easier in America. Also, they made it seem as if money really did grow on trees or something. They made it seem like America was this perfect place and everyone was happy and loved each other. Having a family member in America was a big deal for some people. Everyone talked about how much they wanted to come here and I never knew why. Just looking out that window made me think of all the people that wanted to be here and stand where I was standing.

The next airplane got us to Kentucky. When we came out we saw a Somali family. My little sister ran to them and called one of the women standing there "Mom." She hugged her and everything. We just waited to see her reaction. She turned and told my sister that she wasn't her mom, that the lady next to her was. My mother looked at my sister and smiled at her. My sister had seen pictures of my mother, but Mom had left when she was only six months old. All her life, the closest thing to having a mother had been my grandmother. I don't think that my mother even remembered her. My mother now had a whole new life with our new stepdad and our little brother. She was also pregnant with our little sister. It was an emotional day for all of us. We stayed up all night talking about everything we could. It was a new chapter for all of us. It was the start of something new. My mother had achieved what she had wanted to do for us, which was to give us a better life. A life that she never had. The rest is on us because it depends on what we do with the opportunity. All I want to do is to make her proud and to show her that it was the right thing to do.

In Somalia, when the boys used to play fight, they would say his name—Muhammad Ali—and the winner got to be him. They pretended to be him and wished they were as strong as him. I remember asking about him and they laughed at me and said, "How do you not know about him?"

Muhammad Ali is known in many Muslim countries because he fought for many things and is an example of greatness. Back home, Muhammad Ali was an inspiration to all, he was the light to their darkest day. Even though I never met him in real life, when Muhammad Ali passed away I cried for days. He touched my soul, and when he spoke it was like he was speaking to me. He made me feel like I could do anything in this world.

Years ago I didn't even know that Kentucky existed and now it has become my new home. Now, when I get a call from my family back home and I tell them that I go to the same high school as Muhammad Ali, they don't believe me. Sometimes I can't believe it either. All my life I wanted to meet this man everyone talked about. To end up in his hometown and go to his high school seems like a dream.

Life still has its ups and downs, but it's nothing compared to what I have already faced. If I'd known I would make it out of Somalia and grow up to be this age, I would have been more brave and would have shown more love to my people who didn't make it out alive. I went from nights when I used to pray to God to give me death to nights now when I thank Him for giving me this life.

SORAYA
ROBINSON

COINS IN THE FOUNTAIN

I didn't want to ask anyone for directions, but I also didn't want to look lost. I was new to Central High School and didn't know my way around. I just wanted to find Room 203 to see what the swim coach looked like. All I knew about Central was that they had a bunch of magnet programs. I certainly didn't know they had a swimming pool, so when I and some classmates were sitting on the bleachers in P.E., and a girl with green curly hair made an announcement about the swim team, I was shocked.

"Hey guys! I'm Aaliyah and I'm recruiting people who are interested in joining the swim team!" She told us about a meeting the next week. "Just listen to the announcements, any questions talk to Coach Meador in Room 203." A girl next to me who seemed friendly and nice responded in a goofy manner. "Well, I don't know how to swim, but I do know how to drown," she said.

"Meador will teach you how to swim," Aaliyah said.

I didn't know how to swim either. This was an opportunity to make my wish come true. When I finally found Coach Meador's room, I looked inside

and he was nowhere to be found. The meeting was in less than a week and I couldn't wait to go and get straight into the pool.

I was only allowed to play around in the water growing up. I remember the first time I was given permission to even get into a pool. It was a hot summer morning when I was about eleven. We all woke up sweating and realized we'd forgotten to turn on the air conditioning the night before. My mother went outside, checked the weather, and realized that it was hotter inside than outside. She yelled so loud that it sounded like an echo from each room. "Get dressed! We're going out to get wet." My older brother laughed and ran to the bathroom like his whole life depended on it. I sat on my bed waiting. Moments later my mother popped her head inside my room and said, "Instead of waiting and not doing nothing you can get your clothes ready." I stopped her from walking away and asked if I could get in the pool today since there were only the three of us, which wasn't a lot of people to keep her eyes on. I knew Mom didn't want me to get in pools because she was scared, but I didn't know why.

"I doubt it," she said.

I always had so much excitement for the summertime, and the thing I looked forward to most was going to Algonquin Park where my cousins and I would throw water balloons and play on the big rusty slides and swings that made a clunking noise every time they went up. But when I begged and pleaded to go to the pool my mom would always ask me, "What's the point if you don't know how to swim?" Then she'd tell me to go play around in the sprinklers.

I was dressed in my two piece, we had our towels, and we thought we were ready to go to Algonquin Park, but the pool was closed, and there weren't any surrounding areas where we could use a pool for free either.

That day, we had to think of other water parks that were free in Louisville, so my mom said we would just have to go downtown and play at the park where it was probably cooler anyway. We didn't realize they had a waterpark. When we went downtown, we walked around on the pathway to the park area where we explored and found our way to a sprinkler and a "pool" made from stone. We weren't sure if it was really a pool, but it had numbers carved into the top saying how deep it was, and people were in there, so we sat our stuff down and I started taking off my shorts.

I felt tense chills down my back from my mother's eyes glued on me. I knew there was a small chance of me going swimming—she never let me go—so I sat down. I thought her giving me the look was her way of her saying no. I finally glanced at her and then made eye contact. She said, "You can get inside."

I took off running and didn't look back. I was speeding toward the pool, and I planned to jump inside, but fear, like a shadow, took over me. My hands were sweaty and my body was hot. My thoughts were driving around over and over until I just let go and put my feet into the water. It was a warm, flat feeling as I slowly dropped my body down with only my face out of the water. I was tip-toeing slowly when my brother popped up out of nowhere and splashed me in the face then ran to the end of the pool where it was slightly deeper. I climbed down the hard rock stairs and scraped my knee but kept chasing after him. I went over to where I'd seen a waterfall. I tried to get behind it, but my mother was calling for us because my brother and I had split up and gone too far for her to see us. She called our names for a couple of minutes. I pretended to not hear her voice, but my brother grabbed me and said, "Come on," in a raspy tone.

We grabbed our belongings and our towels and wrapped them around us. On the way to the car I tried hiding from my mom by walking behind her because I felt myself wheezing. I could hear movements of air getting clogged in my lungs. It sounded like a monster and squeaky at the same time. When I tried breathing in, sweat dripped from my forehead and I got dizzy. I closed my mouth so she wouldn't hear me wheezing, but it only made it harder for me to breathe. So I opened my mouth and my wheezing got louder. It sounded like a broken bee and crashing plane. She turned back to me and asked if I was okay.

"I'm fine," I said, still trying to hold onto my breath. She turned back to me again, but this time we stopped walking. She knelt down low to hear me breathing and asked me to take one deep breath. And there it was: I felt a tightness in my heart.

"When we get home you are getting on the breathing machine," she said in a serious tone. I didn't want to get on the breathing machine. I despised the thing. In the car on the way home I lay my head on the head rest and went fast asleep. I was woken up by my mother. I hoped that she'd forgotten, but she hadn't. I walked in the door and I felt my head spinning again. My mother convinced me to take the breathing machine and told me it would make me feel better. I took a shower and lay down, reliving my fun adventure.

Recently, I asked my mom about that downtown pool and the day we went there when we were younger.

"What are you talking about? There's no pool downtown," she said.

When I reminded her of some of the details she said, "Girl, that was no pool. That was a wishing fountain." Then I remembered feeling coins on the bottom of my feet and pretending I was a pirate. A wishing fountain—a well full of wonders and miracles—a place I had not only wished for, but had a vision of for years afterward.

On the day of the swim team meeting, I ran straight there as soon as I heard the bell. There were a handful of people coming and going out of Meador's classroom. I was thinking, "Oh no, I didn't bring my swimsuit or towel or anything." Turns out that people just had big backpacks. People were introducing themselves and trying to get to know each other. I was standing, rocking side to side, waiting for instructions or some type of order. It was 2:31 when he walked in. Coach Meador is Caucasian man who

speaks with a calm but firm tone of voice. He talked about his life and swimming and how he became a coach. He went to DuPont Manual and studied to be a teacher at University of Louisville. Meador swam a lot as a kid and then coached at other clubs and schools. When he came to Central to teach American History, he found out Central had a swimming pool but had cut funding for the swim team. Nobody cared about swimming, he said, but he became the coach and the team has grown over the years. He's met his goal of having a team where everyone feels like they belong, no matter the color of their skin. All you need is the right cap and goggles and swim gear.

There were a handful of people in the room. I didn't think Meador would notice a shy, squirmy kid who was scared to ask questions. I had so many things in my mind that I was just too scared to ask, but each question I developed in my mind he would answer out loud. It was like the man was reading my mind. Meador looked at us and said, "Raise your hand if you don't know how to swim." I looked around. About four people had their hands up. I slowly raised my hand too. He said the most important rule of swimming was DO NOT DIE. Everyone in the room laughed besides two or three people.

I've seen this funny meme that shows this little Black kid sitting in a pool confused and crying. The text above him says, "When you get in the water but remember you Black."

I've thought about where the stereotype "Black people can't swim" comes from. Sixty-four percent of Black people do not know how to swim. Swimming did not become part of the culture for Black people in America. There have been historical events that led up to Black people not learning how to swim. Throughout the Jim Crow era, legislators segregated schools, public parks, theaters, and pools. Black people couldn't swim because they weren't allowed to use the pools. When they did go to pools where whites swam, they were threatened, chased out, or were victims of violence. Later, public funding for pools in urban areas was decreased and people in the suburbs had their own private pools and clubs where they learned how to swim. This continued for generations and, for Blacks, learning how to swim was no longer a part of their upbringing. It wasn't passed down. If your parents don't know how to do something, they probably aren't going to be able to get you to do it.

It's almost like the lack of access brought fear, and one thing that was passed down was this fear of swimming. Even though pools aren't segregated anymore, some Black people don't have the same resources as white folks to be able to swim. In 2019 the city of Louisville closed down four public swimming pools, including the only pool in the West End, making it hard for Black and poor citizens to be able to swim. Today in the West End there are no pools that are free.

I have always heard Black people "can't" swim. It's something we say as a community. But saying you can't do something is a form of negligence that can do so much harm. Can't? That's absolutely ludicrous. This Black person was going to learn how to swim.

After the meeting, I was frightened but so full of joy at the same time. I didn't know what to expect. I felt like I was going to embarrass myself. I didn't like

Saying you can't do something is a form of negligence that can do so much harm.

changes and I knew changes were going to happen to my body and my schedule—and I would have to get my hair wet every day.

I also didn't know how my mother would feel.

I went home that day and told her about the meeting and that I was interested in swimming. The word "attitude" was written all over her face. Finally, she said, "How much will it cost?" I told her it was thirty dollars for the insurance fee. She was going to get my swimsuit from Walmart until I stated that Meador said we would have to get the team swimsuit from Swimville, a store that was a fifty-minute drive from our house. She told me she didn't want to waste her gas and money if I was going to quit like I quit playing the violin. But my playing the violin was something she liked more than I did. This was the first time I actually chose something for myself.

Her black eyebrows shifted downwards. Her golden-brown face looked towards me and the next thing out of her mouth was, "You don't even know how to swim." And she wasn't wrong. But since I was seven years old, I'd always wanted to learn, and my mother had always put her foot down.

"I'm worried that you are going to drown," she said.

When I saw people on the team with the same skin tone as me, I felt like I belonged.

When my grandmother died when I was young, my family all came to Louisville from Chicago and California. At the funeral home, she was in a casket with her arms on top of each other and glorious makeup that made her skin glow. My other cousins and I were in the front lying on this green carpet that looked like grass, praying for Grandma in an upbeat rhythm. After the funeral service it was time to bury my grandmother, and the mood was very dry and gloomy. It took us thirty minutes driving through the graveyard to find where she was going to be buried. It was really hot that day, and my mother's sweaty, salty hand never let go of mine. I saw tons of tombstones. We finally got to my grandmother's spot where we saw a scissor lift lowering her casket into a dried-up hole pruned for the coffin to fit in. We all slowly walked away before seeing the casket being lowered into the dirt.

After we got in the car and drove home, my mother's family was at my house drinking and listening to music. It was a vibe. My cousin La'sha came up to me and said, "Ask your mother if you can go to cousin Tasha's hotel room with us." La'sha's mother said she could go if my mother would definitely let me go. My favorite cousin and I came up with a plan to get both of our parents together, and I asked if I could get in the pool. My mom said she didn't want me to hurt myself or get my hair wet because I had just gotten my hair curled for my grandmother's funeral. She said I could go if I promised I wouldn't get in the pool. Our plan worked, but I made a promise that I eventually did not keep.

My cousins and I were just lying around on the tan covers in the basic tan hotel room. We were hungry, and Tasha said we could eat peanut butter and jelly sandwiches. I didn't like peanut butter so she said, "You can eat those pepperonis in the fridge. Don't be picky." I got mad at Tasha because she left us with no food and nothing to do. We saw there was a pool, so we got some towels and dressed. The pool looked scary, like an abandoned house, but we still jumped in. I couldn't go anywhere deeper than four feet because I couldn't swim. My cousins hopped around the pool and left me to play Marco Polo in the deep end. I couldn't do anything but jump around the pool and float. I was too scared to try.

I had trouble remembering where the pool was for our first practice. It was like going on a wild goose chase until I saw a group of people on the swim team and followed them through the halls. We passed some kids playing volleyball and basketball in the gym, then went through the wrestling room where it smelled like boiled hot dogs. I walked up and yanked the door to the pool room, but it was locked. I looked through the glass and could see the black bleachers and the rectangular pool looking at me. I'd seen a picture of the pool from a long time ago without any water in it, and it looked like a cold, dark skating rink. I stood there for a minute looking onto the giant pool.

The light of the room made the pool look clean, and the pool brightened the room. The water was so blue and clear.

I saw people going down a flight of stairs, so I walked down the steps into the locker rooms. I didn't want to be the first one out, so I waited in the locker room and changed into my gear. You don't need much to swim: a one-piece swimsuit, cap, and goggles. My mother got me an all-black swimsuit with the "Speedo" checkmark printed in white on it. I had a borrowed pair of goggles and a purple cap. After I was dressed, I followed everyone's lead and turned the corner. At the end of a tunnel I opened the door into the pool room and was instantly hit with the dirty coin smell of fresh chlorine. It reminded me of the wishing well.

I was at the pool just waiting to get in when I heard a voice suddenly say, "Get in! What are you waiting for?" Coach Meador seemed much funnier and not as firm as the last time I had seen him. I didn't know what to expect at the start of my first practice. I was scared, but the people around me were so friendly and open. When I saw people on the team with the same skin tone as me, I felt like I belonged.

There were three lanes: one for those who knew how to swim and felt like pros, one for those who needed a little practice, and one for those who had no experience. I got into the lane that related to me. I stuck my leg in and started shivering. The water was so cold that I had to forcefully toss myself in. I ducked down to feel the water against my whole body. The heat in my body went away and I got chills.

I felt like I was in the wrong lane because everyone seemed to have everything under control, to know more than me, to be more experienced than me.

I felt left out and wanted to get out of the pool. I was floating in the water, folded like a pretzel, when Meador told us to get closer so we could hear him talk about the basics of swimming. Meador stood in the middle of the lane and took us step by step, first showing us how to breathe underneath the water by blowing out of our noses, then taking a huge breath through your mouth from the side. He had us practice with our head underneath the water. I didn't know if I was doing it right until I inhaled water through my nose. My nose then burned and I started coughing and sneezing. Everyone turned their eyes on me. We continued practicing breathing.

Later, Meador pulled out these weird-shaped red kick boards and told us to hold on to them from the front. "Kick from your hip," he said, sounding far away. I didn't know what "kicking from your hip"

meant, so I was kicking like I was stomping: picking my knees up and stepping on the water. I was trying my best to move, but it felt like I was staying in the same place and looking like a broken dolphin. But then I felt myself move, just a bit. I went home later and searched YouTube for "how to swim better." I watched some videos on techniques and ways to get better at breathing. On your third stroke you're supposed to take a breath. You blow out of your nose, and breathe in through your mouth for only a second. I tried this as I watched the videos on my phone but made a fool out of myself and had to stop to take normal breaths.

At the second practice, we learned how to use our arms. It seemed so easy when we were watching. I began by placing one arm in front of the other like Meador explained, but bending my elbow when going down. Next, we tried inside the water, so we had to practice our breathing at the same time. We started by going from the beginning of the pool to the end with the kickboard again. I barely made it to the end. I kept on stopping to hold onto the side of the pool. I tried swimming without the kickboard. I could easily move my arms, but I had problems staying on top of the water. I was in the middle of the pool trying to lie flat on the surface but my feet just hit the bottom. I saw my teammates talking like they knew what they were doing. I kept looking around, stopping people while they were swimming and saying, "How do you do that?" Members of the team were so nice and didn't mind showing me how to do something. One girl told me to push off the wall with both of my legs. I pushed off the wall and was "swimming," but only for a few seconds because I got scared and snorted the water again.

Three of my teammates then came to help me. A guy named Andre held me up by pushing me up from my stomach and telling me not to get scared and to keep going.

I was finally kicking and moving my arms and getting comfortable. My teammates told me I had it, that I just needed to stop being scared. I pushed off the wall again and started paddling my feet and tread-milling my arms, then stopped in the middle before I got to the deeper side of the pool. I heard someone say, "Keep going!" but I had to take a breath. I wasn't breathing. I knew how to, but I just wasn't doing it. The coach had said, "Breathe out your nose slightly, making bubbles, and inhale air from out the side before you take your next stroke." I needed to get comfortable with swimming and breathing in water. For months, that's what I did.

I felt out of place and was so ready to give up, but I knew I could do it. It didn't just happen in a day. It took me so long to learn the basics of swimming. By the middle of October, I was finally comfortable swimming, and my breathing got better. When I finally learned, I felt like I'd done something that I had never thought I could do. I was so happy on the inside. My heart always jumped out of my chest at practice. I had literally been scared of water, and now I'm comfortable with being in the water.

Not long ago I was ruminating about a story my mom told me once about the time she rescued my cousin from drowning. She had only told me once, and I never brought it up again because I felt like it would bring her down. But I wanted to know the story of how it happened, and I figured she would tell me how she learned how to swim while we were on the topic.

I walked into her room and tossed myself onto her bed. I smiled at her and she seized a glimpse at me, giggled, then looked down at her phone. I lay back on her bed sideways and she finally took notice of me.

"What do you want?" she said assertively with a smile on.

"Remember when you told me about my cousin almost drowning?" I said.

"You weren't born yet when your cousin almost drowned," she said.

"How did it happen?" I said.

My mother told me that she'd been hanging at the edge of the pool with her feet dangling in the water when she saw my cousins playing around too much. One of them was bouncing up and down, reaching for air. That's when she jumped in to save him.

"I jumped in with my phone and everything," she said. She explained that she got him out and that he was too scared to get back in after that.

"So, who drowned? Nobody?" I said

"It was *my* cousin who drowned in a lake when we were little," she said. She talked about the day and how it all happened. Everyone in the family was at a lake in Chicago for a barbecue. The kids weren't supposed to get in without any adults, but they snuck off and got in and started playing around. When the adults came back, all the children ran out of the lake, but her cousin couldn't swim and went too far out. It was already too late, and when he stopped floating, he was out of reach for a couple of hours.

They used a lake pump to get him out. The last time my mother saw her cousin he was black and blue, like he still retained water inside him. She told me that's why she didn't want me swimming when I was young. Anything could happen. A little accident. That's why she doesn't like for us to be in the pool by ourselves with no one watching.

It was December, and it was time for our first swim meet. I thought the coach had told me that I didn't have to swim in the meet because I wasn't ready. I was still having trouble multitasking. It was either kicking and moving my arms without breathing, or breathing correctly but kicking and moving my arms wrong.

I was sitting up in the bleachers jumping every-where, happy and excited, cheering on my teammates and wishing them good luck when the coach stopped and looked at me through the rail and asked, "Where's your bathing suit?" with a grin and firm look. Meador told me all he needed was a time from me: a record of how long it took me to swim, so that later I could see if I was improving or not. I thought, *Yeah, you can get a time*, but I kept visualizing myself stopping to get out of the water while I was swimming. I'd never done a full lap without stopping, so the idea of doing two felt like a ton of bricks on my shoulder and my stomach was knotted up.

It was time for warmups, and I felt a slight sense of release cooling myself down. I did a full lap without stopping, though I started in the right lane and drifted over into another lane and I got hit in my head by somebody's foot on the way back. I started to overanalyze everything.

It was my time to swim. My heart was racing, and I didn't have the strength to do it. I stood behind the diving board. As I heard the first long beep that tells you to get ready, I thought I was going to make a fool out of myself by diving into the pool before everybody else. The three beeps went fast, but it felt like I was moving in slow motion as I turned both ways to make sure it was time to go. I got myself into the water by doing a normal jump from the edge of the pool. I pushed my myself into the water then took my head out to take my first stroke.

I was in the middle of the pool, getting ready to give up. I couldn't breathe at my normal pace. I wanted to cry and my jaw was clenching. My legs tightened up. Every stroke was a loss of breath. My attempt to do a flip and turn after my first lap was a fail, and I had one more full lap to go. The other swimmers were already out of the pool. I then stopped kicking my legs because they finally gave up and tensed up fully. I just moved my arms. I hit the mark close to the endpoint and started kicking with my knees.

I finally reached the end. I was the last one. I felt so disappointed when I got out of the pool, but everyone was clapping and cheering. Meador said he was still proud of me even though my time was nearly three minutes. I was shocked that I had even done it.

Swimming still isn't easy for me. When I was younger, I didn't have the satisfaction of being in the pool because of the panic in my mom's heart and because there were problems finding pools to go to. I couldn't swim because I didn't have the resources to swim until I joined the swim team. Now, during the school year, I'm in the pool three or four days a week.

Swimming is an individual sport, but also a team sport. When you spend time in the pool together and at meets, you cheer each other on and push each other. I love being in the pool. Swimming has taught me that, sometimes, to be comfortable, first I have to be uncomfortable, and that it's okay to be uncomfortable. To lose my fear, I need to let loose and learn to control my emotions. Working under pressure is something I'm still learning, but I've learned how to do something I didn't think I could do.

MELISA
TORRES ROJAS

ORGULLOSA Y FIERA

When the automatic doors open at Walmart, it's like walking into a paradise. The temperature is always perfect. Cool rainy days are forgotten in the heat of the store. Freshness is in the air as the sprinklers graciously spray the greens in the produce section. The pop music coming and going in the background keeps my family's pace. There are so many products lined up one after the other that it's distracting. The flawless skin of the tomatoes brings me closer to a greater contemplation of the neatly placed juice bottles. Walmart is the center of simplicity in the life we live now.

Posters hang from the ceiling that hint at the categories of foods in each aisle, but we've memorized the map of our most used items. Out of all the aisles, though, the Hispanic section means home, from the names of the products to the familiar tastes that water my mouth. I know the Bustelo coffee is at the end of the aisle. That yellow can with a red banner at the bottom is my mom's fuel every day. The boxes of fruit juice have the word GOYA written in capital letters on a label that is light blue, like the waters of the Caribbean. And lastly, in that aisle, Mom picks up a yellow, dark pink, and orange box of saffron that she will use to make yellow rice, paellas, fricassee, soups, meat in sauce with potatoes, and stews. Aisle by aisle

the shopping cart gets more and more full. We can eat avocados and tomatoes even when they are not in season, and there is always enough bread, oil, and rice, unlike the scarcity that defines Cuba.

This Walmart is in one of the most diverse parts of Louisville. My sister and I guess the ethnicity of people across the bakery and vegetable zones. I can tell who the Cubans are even if they are not speaking a word. Cubans tend to have a different fashion than other Latin American countries. Most men wear tight shirts, gold chains, jeans, and sneakers. One of the men excluded from that common fashion is my father. Many confuse him with being Mexican. He doesn't get mad. There is absolutely nothing wrong with being Mexican. In addition, Cuban men like to coordinate the color of their shirt with the color of their shoes or jeans and wear a lot of eau de parfum that lasts for hours with a few sprays. As for the women, most wear gold accessories and leggings in combination with sneakers. It's also easy to tell because I listen to the accent, of course. Even though there are numerous accents within Cuba, in general we sound as fast as a locomotive.

Nowhere in Cuba can you find a place as complete as Walmart. Back in Holguin, Cuba, where I'm from, food and other essentials were limited.

When things arrived at the bodega, people would run to quickly form a long queue. "The soap arrived!" a neighbor would say, and the line would get longer by the second. It was never guaranteed that you would get what you came for by the time you got to the front of the line.

But most of what we consume in the U.S. has preservatives or it's frozen. By the time the food reaches our mouths, it has lost most of its flavor. The lack of truly fresh vegetables and fruits and the limited socialization with the people of the community makes me wish we had more local fresh food and a more social community like we did back in Cuba. People talked to each other more. From early in the morning, doors were wide open. Grandparents stayed home while children went to school and adults worked. People sat on their porches so others would stop and talk for a while. I miss the constant in and out of houses, and the sound of bicycle bells and loud music at any hour of the day. Throughout the streets of my neighborhood, many people would make homemade snacks to sell out of their own houses.

My neighbor Araceli made and sold mantecados, shortbread cookies with circles of guava jam in the middle of them. My paternal great-grandma used to sell mango, strawberry, and banana ice cream bars. She doesn't sell them anymore, but one of her sons has a small market stall on the front porch right where my grandpa Eduardo used to sell meat, fruits, and vegetables. We used to buy yogurt from a nearby neighbor. Instead of buying mayonnaise, my grandma made it.

Here in Louisville, my cousin Yandy grows aji cachucha peppers in his backyard. These sweet peppers come in green, red, orange, and light yellow colors and look shiny and wrinkled, like closed flowers with thin green stems. This pepper is famous in Cuban cuisine, and Yandy gifts them to my mom. The aroma around the house reminds my soul of memories it had forgotten. The first day she brought them home, Mom's face lit up when she began to cook. As I sat at the dining table doing my pre-calculus homework, Mom began to chop the gifts of the earth to add them to the yellow rice she was preparing. Right after the knife cut through the pepper, the sweet and earthy aroma rose into the air and made its way into my nose. I looked up in less than a second and a smile took over my face. "Mamiii!! Is it what I think it is?!" She laughed and said, "Meli, the aji cachucha has returned to our home."

I remember running through our neighborhood in Cuba with all my friends and hearing pressure cookers spread the smell of the peppers. The rich aroma would escape through the opened doors and windows of every house. My farmer cousin Rafael used to bring sacks of produce from the farm to sell in the city. Many of the sellers like him gathered in one of the main streets and sold from

morning to afternoon. Rafael used a wheelbarrow to present his produce. He sold everything from cachucha peppers to corn to tomatoes to plantains to beans. It all depended on the season. "Peppers! Pepperrrrrrrssssssss!" he yelled. On one side, vendors sold ice cream along with popcorn and Cuban pizza. Throughout the day the horse-drawn carriages stopped to unload and reload passengers. By the end of the day the streets drowned in puddles of water mixed with urine and feces from the horses, and the trash bags held less trash than the streets.

When I lived in Cuba, I imagined the U.S. as a paradise where everything was perfect. "I am sure there are no unpainted buildings over there and the streets are sparkly clean," I said to my best friend one day. In my little head, I saw no homelessness. I saw no economic problems like we had in Cuba. Papá

says that from a young age he began to notice that the socialist system did not work. "The long speeches Fidel Castro gave did not change my opinion, because at the end of the day," he told me, "what I saw on the plate did not reflect anything that he said. I would watch American movies and the stores looked so packed, like nothing I had ever seen. When my uncle came to visit from the United States, I asked him how things were, and he said they had everything. No scarcity at all."

My dad has explained how, in 1991, when the USSR dissolved and ended relations with Cuba, this caused a drastic change in the economy of the island. This time—known as "El Período Especial," or The Special Period—brought a series of limitations to Cuba, the most significant ones being limitations of food and transportation. Since the USSR had been responsible for the majority of the imported oil in Cuba, there was now only 10% of the oil that had been available pre-1990s, so agriculture decreased because the tractors needed oil. Like a domino effect, it caused a widespread food shortage.

Papá recalls that food was so scarce that everyone's favorite snack was bread with brown sugar as the spread. The government had the bodegas distribute the food in rations per household. The kids were the only ones to receive milk. The meat portion was counted exactly. The bread became so hard that the best option was to toast it on the pan with a drop of the little oil the bodega distributed. No one had another option because private businesses weren't allowed at that time.

When my parents were young, students from seventh to twelfth grade all across Cuba were required to attend "la escuela al campo," or "field school." Mom would spend forty-five days during summer break working in the fields. Most of the time she collected coffee and tomatoes.

When food was scarce in the cafeteria of field school, the teachers asked farmers around the area if they could exchange labor from students in their fields for food. From early in the morning till late afternoon, sweaty faces worked in the field. "Today, each person needs to pick eight big cans of coffee seeds," shouted the teacher. "AND, I don't want to see anyone milking the trees," exclaimed the teacher. Milking is a way to describe the way many students collected the coffee. Just like milking a cow, the students would pull down the branches, which caused the tree to lose the immature coffee seeds, too.

When the food scarcity period was announced by the government, the cafeteria stopped giving

bacon, and replaced it with eggs and white rice. Sometimes they would give fish. All the students were given a card that marked when they were served in the cafeteria.

In his athletics boarding high school, my papá would erase the checkboxes to get a second helping because the food they provided wasn't enough anymore. At the beginning, enough food had been given to satisfy the athletes—except beef, which was prohibited in all corners of the country. The prohibition is still present today, but it has never been about religious purposes. The Cuban government implemented the rule because cows are only supposed to be used for milking.

Along with the food scarcity came power outages that lasted an average of sixteen hours a day during the '90s. My mom and dad vividly remember these.

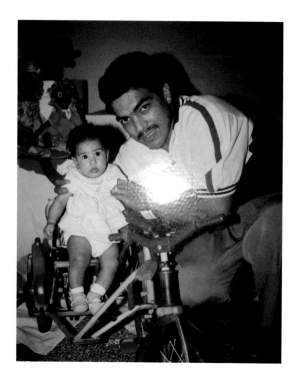

I only had a short taste of the power outages compared to them. My mom told me that when I was born in 2003, my grandfather put together a fan with batteries so that I would have air in the heat of the nights. One hot night when I was around four, the fan had no batteries and our sweating made it impossible to fall asleep. Mom and Grandma took turns waving either a flamenco hand-fan or a newspaper to provide me and my sister with some breeze. As I closed my eyes—in and out of sleep—I heard the back and forth of the newspaper and I would think, "Poor Grandma, her hand must be so tired, but this breeze feels so nice."

The scarcity trained the Cuban community, including me, to value everything. "Reusing and creating" is the approach that allowed my family to stay afloat. We reused any plastic containers for storage and used the toothpaste tube all the way to the point of cutting it with scissors to scrape the paste out. But, I remember more joyous moments than sad ones. I know that my parents had it rough and they have made sacrifices for my sister and me to have a better future. More than anything, that is my greatest motivation to work hard to study for a career that I will enjoy and that will at the same time provide me with a comfortable income. That will allow me to help them live comfortably with no worries about rent, money, or hospital costs.

"Hey. Get three gallons of milk," my mom demanded as the four of us walked through Walmart. "They are cheaper here."

After going back and forth for a while, Papá jokingly commented, "I am done with people controlling me. No one is going to control me."

"Well, you sure had four years of total independence." I didn't think before I blurted this out, but as soon as I said it, I felt a sudden relief fill my entire body. I guess I had never told Papá how much I had missed and needed him during those years. This feeling of relief was unfamiliar because I had social anxiety. When I went to the store I usually felt like everyone was judging me just by the way I looked or talked, so to be able to let go of such toxic thoughts and be present with my dad in the moment really meant a lot. It was a step toward becoming the person I wanted to become.

Papá laughed and said, "Don't exaggerate, it was only two and a half years."

"Are you counting the two times you came to visit for a month during 2008 and 2009?" I asked.

"Yes," he replied.

"Papá," I softly sighed, "That doesn't count as living and coexisting. We didn't live together from 2008 to 2012." All of that came out of me. Again, it felt unfamiliar because I have the habit of over-thinking before speaking.

Papá took it as a joke and we all continued shopping. I don't know if he has thought about it since that day, but I have found myself reflecting on my childhood, and I realize that I had been holding off that feeling of regret for not having him for such an important stage in my life. I love my mother and everything that she has sacrificed to guide us and give my sister and me a comfortable life, but before he left, I was really close to Papá.

Papá, with thick, straight, black hair like a race-horse's. Since I was small, his coffee-colored eyes would invite me into his strong soul. No matter how far apart we were, the memory of his eyes was retained in my memory. I followed him everywhere he went. If he didn't want me to go with him, he'd say, "Are you sure you want to go? I am going to the dentist." I had always been terrified of the dentist.

But I loved exploring as I sat comfortably in the tiny wooden seat screwed into the bar of the bicycle Papá pedaled around Holguin for everything. As the bicycle went through narrow streets where no cars could fit, every door and window of every house we passed was open. The air was filled with colonial and modern vibes and smelled like worn out walls and fresh paint. The tall ceilings of the colonial homes contrasted the low and flat style of the modern buildings.

Papá also rode his bike to medical school, where he studied to become a family doctor. He graduated

third in his class and still came home from the clinic on a bicycle. "I just don't understand," he would sigh. "How am I struggling after so much hard work? Those that only went to school so they could eat the school lunch are economically better off than me." My dad carried the weight of worry on his shoulders. Worries for the future of my mom, my sister and me, worries about the bills. Worries that, to this day, have not allowed him to sit for a second to think of the time that has passed.

When Papá became a doctor he could have chosen a specialty, but he decided to accept a place in a medical mission to Venezuela. On the day he left for Venezuela in 2008 he gave me a hug as tight as the muscles of a racehorse, and took a briefcase full of dreams. I didn't know how much my life would change without him.

Since the 1970s, the Cuban government has been sending doctors to help countries in need of medical professionals. "It's a business for the government," Papá told me. "Cuba sends doctors to countries who need help. They pay the Cuban doctors very little and the rest is given to the Cuban government." The Cuban government gives the "privilege" of free college and university education, but the truth is that they squeeze professionals to the last drop without compassion. My dad only got $100 out of the $4,000 the Venezuelan government actually paid. Venezuela also provided Cuba with petroleum.

Many doctors who left on missions already had families. Leaving meant that their families would prosper, but it also meant that they wouldn't have the chance to cultivate memories with their children. Venezuela was the path to Papá's hopes and bigger dreams he had in mind, but when he left on his mission our lives were never the same.

When he arrived in Venezuela he had to work even harder than he had worked in Cuba. The small clinic that he attended was a small house turned into a "consultorio" where Papá consulted with patients who had problems with hypertension, diabetes, and other chronic illnesses. From there he advised them and referred them to specialists. In the afternoon, it was time to visit the patients in their houses to give preventive talks and bring them their prescriptions. Apart from his responsibilities as a doctor and working during the night, he had to teach biochemistry to medical students and sleep in a bunk bed in a house with fourteen people. Papá recalls, "The doctors native to Venezuela would work in the advanced hospitals with good conditions, while the mission doctors were sent to the rural areas where the gangs were concentrated. Compared to Cuba, the violence was ten times greater." Unlike the island, people in Venezuela owned guns.

Papá told me about how he constantly heard news of doctors being killed for things like a thin gold chain around their necks.

After some advice from Venezuelan friends, I carried a little money in my wallet because if they tried to rob you and you didn't have anything they could also kill you. I did not own any jewelry except for a plastic watch. I had a tiny phone and if they saw it they would be like, "No way, bro, I have a better one than that." This one day I was riding my bicycle up a steep hill where I had to slow down, and before I knew it, two members of a gang came up to me to rob my bicycle.

"Give me the bicycle!" they demanded.

"What did you say?" I asked, knowing what the question was.

"Give me the bike," one of the robbers replied.

"Oh I can't, this bicycle belongs to my cousin."

"I don't care if it belongs to your cousin."

By that time I had calculated that the robbers didn't have a gun. So when they came towards me, one grabbed the wheel of my bike. Thanking God for the seven years of judo I took back in Cuba, I did a Sumi-otoshi, throwing one of them to the side, and then I hit the other one with the bike. I ended up losing my tiny phone because it fell out of my pocket. That was the only thing they took.

Right after the incident, I headed to play baseball with some friends from el barrio, and I told them what happened. I found out that one of my friends and a patient from the clinic was the jefe of the gang of the barrio. Once I told the group what happened, my friend called the jefe from the barrio on the other side. He said,

"Look, I don't want problems with you. We have been in peace for several months now. But two of your men took the doctor's phone. Bring it to him if you don't want problems with me."

Later that week the nurse gave me my tiny phone, saying that someone had brought it in.

I had no idea that one of my patients had that power in the neighborhood. I was blessed to have such protection while I was over there.

After a year in Venezuela, Papá came home to visit for a month. When I saw the military-green jeep parked outside, I knew it was Papá. He surprised my sister and me with the cutest stuffed animals and snacks with packaging so beautiful that we saved them after eating what was inside. I knew he hadn't come back forever, that he would leave promptly. The hardest thing for me was realizing that we weren't as close anymore. *Of course that's my dad, the one who used to come home sweaty in his white coat, the one who took me everywhere with him, but why am I so shy around him?* I asked myself, wanting that feeling to change as quickly as possible. I wanted everything to go back to the way it was.

During his visit we went to visit the rural area high up in the mountains of El Culebro where we lived before my sister was born. The majagua azul is a tree with large, strong trunks, and the wood produced by these beasts was unique. Papá had always thought that these trees were beautiful and dreamt of turning them into beds and a dinner table. Papá's work in Venezuela allowed him to afford to pay a carpenter to make two bed frames and a large dining table from this wood. When the table and beds arrived, I thought they were the most beautiful I had ever seen, and the varnish smell filled the house, so it felt like the once huge tree was present in my house. It is incredible to me that today, after almost ten years, the table still looks new.

After Papá left, he called us and sent us clothes. I will forever be grateful for Papá's hard work and for the concern he always had for us and for our future. I didn't know we wouldn't see him for two and a half years. I wished that he could have taken me to my first day of school, eaten dinner with me, helped me learn the multiplication tables, and taught me how to ride a bicycle. He left right before I began preschool, and it was challenging for me to adapt to school.

Grandma walked with me to school in the morning, and when she left me there my stomach and throat had knots in them. "Abuelita, you are going to come back, right?" I would ask her while giving her a tight hug. The more she distanced herself from the building, the more watery my eyes got. I felt like I was stuck in a prison. The thought of being there for hours felt like an eternity. I was scared of my teacher, who used to pull the girls' hair and hit the boys in the face.

Through the windows of my school you could see Moskviches going up and down the road, along with bicycles, horse carriages, and pedestrians with large umbrellas. Every first grader in the school plaza was wearing impeccable uniforms. With their right hands to their foreheads, they said, "Pioneers for Communism! We will be like the Che." At the time I had no idea what it meant. Thinking back now, I see how they began to indoctrinate young minds with communist statements, and that I was part of their project.

At the end of the day, I would look through the holes of the brick wall by the front gate of the pre-school building and watch my friends' fathers pick them up. I would wish to see my dad's magical smile peek through the iron gates to pick me up in his green Chinese Flying Pigeon bicycle. I also missed his hugs. I knew how they felt because he never forgot to give me one as soon as he arrived home from work. In that way I was lucky, and I didn't know it.

But most of the time it was my Grandpa Maximo who would pick me up from school on the bicycle that Dad left to him. Along the way home the pizza stations on the side of the road invited us with the amazing smell. "Pizza, pizza, get your pizza! Only five pesos!" Cuban pizza is thick like pan pizza, but it is baked individually in the size of an average plate and they fold it in half so you can pick it up with your hands.

The stretchy cheese bites were accompanied by a refreshing guava shake. When we would get home, Grandma would have a pressure cooker on the stove, maybe making chícharo. I would take a shower and do my homework enthusiastically then go outside to play with other kids like my best friend, Juanki. He is the brother I never had. We were born a month apart, and we slept in the same crib as tiny babies. Up until the day I left Cuba we hung out every single day, playing with other kids in the narrow and imperfect pavement of our barrio, running from end to end while we played el topa topa, or tag. The most vivid moments of those games were unfortunately when we got hurt. If we landed like an airplane with our hands and knees on the dusty floor, the whole neighborhood knew it; like the sound of a siren we cried a continuous sound that didn't stop until we felt

the comfort of our grandparents. Then the fun ended because our families would say, "I told you to stop running. Now look what happened to you. I don't want to see you running for the rest of the day."

And that's when the party ended. The group disintegrated. Everyone went to their house to shower and eat and then gathered again in any place where the neighbors wouldn't kick us out for talking too loud. The neighbors would pop their heads out of the wide open doors of their houses. "Guys, be quiet, we are watching the television here."

The only thing that could prevent us from hanging out was getting grounded. So sad, those days. When it was me, Juanki would come visit me through the locked iron gate. It felt like I was the prisoner who was being visited by their tightest friend. My homie. When Juanki was grounded, I had to travel up the stairs to get to the side of his house that had windows, where we talked until his dad would tell me to go back home because Juanki wasn't allowed to talk to anyone. I would go back home sad and be bored for the rest of the day, having to stay inside while everyone took the siesta after lunch. Mom would close the door to the house and throw one arm over her eyes while she lay with Mari beside her on a twin bed in the living room. Meanwhile, Grandpa Maximo would be knocked out in the rocking chair and Grandma Irma would be on her bed. Everyone would sleep, but I couldn't close my eyes. To kill time, I would read books that my paternal grandma Aida bought me at book fairs. From time to time I would cry a little inside, wishing I could be playing outside.

One day as I was running through the neighborhood with Juanki, Mom called me into our room. The sky was clear and the sun could break rocks. I came into the house suffocated. The sweat rolled down the side of my forehead and I was wearing a pink shirt with The Chipmunks on it. Mom was calm and sitting on the edge of the bed.

"We have to travel to Havana next week. You have to help me with your sister because we are traveling alone."

"Why do we have to go?"

"I just talked to your dad. We are starting the interview process at the U.S. Embassy in Havana. In a couple of months, we might be living in the U.S.," she responded, looking deeply into my eyes. "Don't tell anyone about it."

My Papá had quit the mission suddenly and defected. He had been planning to visit Cuba but began to

We hung out every single day, playing with other kids in the narrow and imperfect pavement of our barrio.

suspect that a superior nurse wanted to send him back to Cuba indefinitely. "Since the first day I arrived, he disliked me," Papá told me. "Thank God I didn't share that I was planning to fly to Cuba because he would have sent a letter to our superiors to cancel my mission and I would have been trapped there."

On a Monday morning Papá asked a superior nurse for permission to go to another city to buy clothes for my sister and me because they were cheaper over there. "He pulled me aside so that my other co-workers wouldn't hear me asking for permission. As I was buying the clothes, another superior called me and asked me to return because I had not asked for permission. They told me to be back in an hour or I'd be in trouble, but the town was two hours away." After dad went back to the clinic, he overheard the two superiors saying, "We are going to trap him." Having heard that, Papá was awakened to their intentions. "Later that day," he told me, "I received a message from the superior saying that there was a meeting Wednesday and for everyone to bring their passports.

"I knew that if I went to the meeting, they would confiscate my passport and I would be trapped forever. I had to decide quickly. I knew that leaving meant I would never be able to enter Cuba again. But, before my future, I thought of you two," my dad told me.

"If you guys studied in Cuba, there was no future." Leaving the mission was a once in a lifetime chance. Papá looked into the future for his family, even if he could never return to the island that saw him grow. Papá knew that if he got to the U.S. he could begin the process to ask for Mom, my sister, and me, and that we would be reunited in six or seven years.

"I didn't go to the meeting. I packed my things and left the house. Later that same day, the Venezuelan owner of the house informed me that military personnel from the Cuban state security dressed in civilian clothes had come asking for me, saying that they were my friends. The owner told me that they arrived in a jeep and as they were getting back into the car he saw their guns. If the military personnel would have found me, they would have taken me directly to the airport to go back to Cuba."

For eight months Papá worked in a senior home in Venezuela. In that time he got help from a program called Barrio Afuera: *out of the neighborhood.* (The Cuban mission was called Barrio Adentro, or *inside the neighborhood.*) Barrio Afuera helped him apply for the Cuban Medical Professional Program, implemented by President Bush, that allowed Cuban doctors and their families to come to the U.S.

Papá sold everything he'd bought to send to Cuba and used that money to immigrate to the U.S. "I took a bus from Venezuela to Colombia that traveled through mountain roads so close to precipices that my forehead was sweating," he told me. "Since I had hundreds of dollars with me, I put them inside of my belt and my socks because along the way these buses got stopped by malandros—robbers and gangsters. It was hard to fall asleep. From Bogotá, Colombia I took the airplane to Miami, Florida, where I reunited with my uncle who had left Cuba in the '70s. It was a rebirth for me when I stepped foot in this beautiful country, but I would learn that Florida was too expensive, there was a scarcity of jobs, and that the majority of jobs paid very little compared to what the rents demanded. I packed up my bag and went to Texas to work at the oil refineries. Within a year I was able to get you guys to the U.S. legally. It was quicker than I ever anticipated. I came with the mindset that the process would take at least six years. It was a blessing on so many levels from the time I stepped foot in Venezuela all the way to being able to arrive safely in the U.S., which is a journey many dream of completing and few achieve. I have incredible respect for those who have traveled through harsher circumstances, through the ocean and through land."

After arriving in Florida, he was transferred to Houston, Texas, where Catholic Charities welcomed him and helped Papá with the information he needed to claim us. The Cuban Medical Professional Parole Program was so powerful that Papá did not even have to wait two years until he became a U.S. resident to claim us. Incredibly, Mom, my sister, and I were on American soil seventeen months after Papá arrived in the United States.

When Mom sat me down in the kitchen that day and told me we were leaving, my mind was still processing it, but I nodded. I had no idea what it felt like to leave the country. I went outside to talk with Juanki in the shadow of an almond tree which was our air-conditioner in the heat of the day. Once I saw Juanki, I felt this peace. I decided not to tell him anything because it felt surreal to think of the

possibility of ever saying goodbye to him. We sat and talked about the unknown and, like we did in most of our conversations, what the U.S. was like. He told me that the streets are clean and there is a 24/7 cartoon channel. We drew in the dirt with a stick and silence took over, but it wasn't awkward. My mind was still with my mom's words: *Don't tell anyone. We might be leaving soon to the United States.* I agreed with her because close to our house lived the president of CDR, the Comites de Defensa de la Revolución, which was the eyes and ears of the Revolution. Any counter-revolutionary activity was to be reported by the CDR. Before the '90s, Cubans who left the island were looked at as traitors by other Cubans. The CDR would encourage people to throw eggs and shout insults towards those who decided to leave. But the mentality of people changed once many Cubans won the visa lottery under the Diversity Visa Program and the U.S.-Cuba Migration Accord of 1994. Now the majority of the island residents saw those that left as people who wanted to prosper and be in the advanced world. At the time I didn't know that nothing would have happened if the CDR would have found out about our upcoming trip.

My heart was split in half. I would miss my neighborhood, my family, and Juanki. But I would be able to hug my dad and finally feel the divine American atmosphere. And even if every time Juanki looked into my eyes I felt the pressure of telling the news to my best friend, I didn't. He wouldn't find out until the same morning we were leaving.

My grandma called out into the neighborhood and I went inside to shower and eat.

The idea of leaving the country came back to me as we were eating. I didn't even need to ask Grandma what she thought. She looked worried. Mom was her only child and they had always been super close. For my sister and me, Grandma and Grandpa were like another mother and father. My strong abuelita Irma said, with the sweetest smile yet a worried look, "You guys need to be close to your daddy. He will take care of you better than anyone. Don't worry about us."

Later that night I could hear Mom and her talking through the sound of the fan. They were planning the trip to Havana. I could already feel my stomach turning upside down from the long ride we were about to take, and it began to hurt every night. The morning of the trip I told my grandma, "I don't feel good, Abuelita."

"It's better that you don't eat anything," she advised. "Here, take this lemon and smell it if you start to feel nauseous," she said. I had butterflies in my stomach. I had inherited my dad and grandmother's motion sickness, and I knew what was waiting for me. Before the bicycle taxi arrived, I sat next to Abuelita in the living room and gently laid down my head on her cold arm. She got a menthol bottle and applied some on my belly in the form of a cross, then she gave me a kiss on the forehead, reminding me to keep my head against the seat of the bus at all times.

It looked like time hadn't passed in Havana. The paint on the buildings had been the same for who knows how long. Most of the iron parts were oxidized from the air that comes from the ocean. The more we went into the city the darker the streets seemed.

Havana gave me a solitary vibe. There was barely anyone driving, walking, or riding a bicycle along the pier at El Malecon—the stone seawall that stops big waves in the port of Havana.

The United States Embassy was across the street from the pier. The day of the interview was pretty calm. The sky was clear and the salty and humid wind moved my hair in all directions. I wore a jacket for the air conditioner blowing inside. I wasn't nervous, but Mom was. Her hands were as cold as a glass of ice. When we sat down for the interview, our interviewer spoke Spanish, but with a very American accent. I don't recall what he asked Mom, yet he did ask me two questions: Do you want to go to the U.S.? Do you miss your dad?

"Without a doubt." I said. "Yes to both."

The man smiled and said, "Have a nice trip" in Spanish. We headed out of the office with a lot of hope. It was a step closer to seeing Papá.

Compared to other cases ours was super quick. Not everyone has the luck to have a parent claim you through The Cuban Medical Professional Parole Program. Even though my dad had defected from his mission, Mom, my sister, and I didn't get into any trouble.

For the next six months life changed back in Holguin. I knew I was going to leave my friends who had been with me since kindergarten. Papá recommended that I take English classes, but nothing stuck. I just couldn't. Everything sounded the same. Even though the day of departure was getting closer, I decided not to worry and have fun with my friends and family. Before I knew it, Grandma and Mom were packing, then the day of our flight had finally arrived.

Grandma, Grandpa, and other family members took us to the international airport in Holguin. I held Grandma's hand and rested my head on her cold arm until we arrived. I thought it was the last time I would ever see them. With goosebumps all over my body, I suddenly woke up to reality and gave everyone hugs and many, many kisses. When we crossed the double doors into the airport, we couldn't go outside anymore. My grandparents were now too far to reach. There was no way to go back. I would have to swim. It felt like a dream. I didn't know how to feel.

It was my first time flying in an airplane and my anxiety increased when the plane started to speed up. I wasn't used to the air conditioner and wearing sandals didn't help. I was between Mom and Mari, drinking apple juice to calm myself. Mari was not scared to look out the window and even went to sleep. The best part of the experience was seeing Miami from above. The city seemed to be organized and colorful. It felt like I had time-traveled to the future I saw in movies. The perfect geometric shapes of the city from the airplane seemed so unrealistic to me.

When an officer at the airport asked for our passports, mom's sweaty hand told me how nervous she was; she didn't understand any of what the officer had said. Thankfully someone in the line helped translate. When I saw my aunt Teresa, uncle Frank, and my cousin Anthony, I was so glad to see something familiar. They had brought us two stuffed bunnies which we loved and still have. When we got in my aunt's car, the combination of perfume and the car moving turned my stomach and this time I couldn't keep from vomiting. Thankfully there was a plastic bag I could use, so the car did not suffer. But my stomach and heart didn't feel complete. I missed my grandparents and the whole family was left behind, and I would be lying if I said it was easy to adapt to one of the best countries in the world.

We settled in Florida for a month before Papá came from Texas where he was working. When he finally arrived at the front gate of mom's aunt's apartment where we were staying, I rushed out to him with butterflies in my stomach and hugged him so tightly. Working overtime at night had made him look different. He had bags under his eyes and his face wasn't tight anymore, but his smile remained. Papito's face was really in front of me. Was it a dream or was it real? I had a knot in my throat. A completely new chapter began that day, and I will forever cherish that moment. That night, I could once again take dad's shoes off and bring him his slippers. With a good night hug for the first time in a long time, I said, "Hasta mañana, Papá." I knew that I was so lucky to have such amazing parents.

The next morning, my eyes were still closed when I heard a familiar voice. I approached the kitchen where everyone was and felt a little shy to see my dad again. Yet, when he said, "Mi cochichi de papito—good morning, my bella," I got emotional. But I kept it together and gave him a hug. That day, we went to Miami Beach. My dad had gotten an advertisement from the Newport Beachside Hotel saying that they were giving out free breakfast, lunch, and dinner and access to their pool. On the drive we listened to the radio, and I specifically remember listening to "We Found Love" by Rihanna. That song always brings me back to 2012, the year that I will never forget.

I had no idea what to expect of a Florida beach, but the palm trees across the city got me excited. I

was already astonished by all the meticulously clean streets when we pulled up to the grandiose hotel. It was the most luxurious thing I had ever seen. My mom, my sister, and I were admiring the pool and the palm leaves that moved from side to side with the salty wind as my dad talked to the front desk. We could see the beach and the pool, and it was like nothing could go wrong, until it did. All of a sudden we were on a high floor attending a "timeshare conference." Papá didn't know about it until he got there. But it couldn't take that long, right? We arrived at the hotel at 9:00 a.m. and sat in that conference until 3:00 p.m. Six hours sitting and admiring other people having fun. Maria and I should have won a medal for Most Patient Children in America: Ages Five to Eight. Papá left the timeshare conference owning one of the timeshares. I guess that's why the U.S. is the #1 economy in the world. They really know how to attract people, and convince them, and drive them crazy to the point of buying.

We finally got to the beach. We played in the sand and took pictures. In the busyness of waves I forgot the life I left in Cuba. I had talked to my grandparents the night before. I had confirmed that they were okay, and I just wanted to enjoy the moment with my family. Later, we headed up a short set of stairs to enjoy the pool. When we lived in Cuba, citizens weren't allowed to enter hotels or pools easily. Very, very few had the money for such luxury. There was a part of me that didn't know how to enjoy a pool. There was barely anyone that looked like us. I feared getting in trouble even though I knew there wasn't a chance of that happening. And on top of that I didn't know how to swim. But we went several more times for the six months we lived in Hialeah, Florida, and I felt more confident each time.

It was too dark in the auditorium to read, but there was enough light to see my dad's pure smile.

Later we moved to Texas and, with some guidance from one of his friends and certification from a community college back in Texas, Papá got a job as a medical assistant at University of Louisville Hospital. My dad hopes to practice medicine in the U.S., just not as a doctor. Right now he is a medical assistant and is studying to become a registered nurse, and later he will study to upgrade to nurse practitioner. He decided to stay in the medical field because it is what he studied and helping sick people is what he likes to do. He tells me, "It is very hard for me to find a job because hospitals prefer recently graduated doctors. I graduated seventeen years ago. The irony is that I have more years of experience, but they are years of experience outside the U.S."

I have also decided to pursue a career in medicine. Coming from a really small school district in Texas with four middle schools and two high schools, I couldn't believe the many high school options in front of me. Central High School stood out to me for its pre-med magnet, though. But getting into Central didn't automatically guarantee me a place in the pre-med magnet. In freshman year everyone explores the magnets in a "magnet rotation" before choosing which one they want to attend for the rest of high school. Each magnet rotation took a week, and it took most of the year to go through them all. I was super excited and nervous when I finally reached the pre-med magnet. This was my chance to show the teacher why I had come to Central.

Right away, she gave us a sheet that included abbreviations for Latin names of terms used on medical sheets and prescriptions. On the last day of rounds we'd be tested on things like: a.d.: *auris dextra* = right ear, a.s.: *auris sinister* = left ear, or, p.o.: *per os* = by mouth. We were only required to learn the Latin abbreviation and the definition of the term. Looking at the sheet, I said to myself, *Melisa, you need to stand out. But how?* I decided that I would also learn the whole Latin name as well as the abbreviation and definition.

The day of the test, when I finished what was required of me and had some time left, I got a piece of paper and began writing down the Latin words from memory. But when the teacher came by to pick up my test, she saw the scratch paper containing the Latin words and said, "Are you cheating?" My heart was running a 100 meter sprint as I had to awkwardly explain to her that I'd written them by memory, and that I had memorized the Latin words in addition to the abbreviations and definitions." She looked at me with distrust, and from that day until the interview a month later, I had really bad anxiety every time I thought about the encounter.

The day of the interview finally arrived, and I just wanted to get it over with so the butterflies would migrate from my stomach. I dressed professionally with a red and black dress and short heels I was barely able to walk in. When I entered the auditorium at Central on the day of the pre-med magnet interviews, it was full of a hundred brilliant students who were applying for only thirty available spots.

I was so intimidated and the setup in the auditorium only made it worse. Those waiting sat on the audience seats and the ones being interviewed had to ascend the stairs to the stage where the bright lights faced them. While I was sitting in the second row of the middle section at the auditorium, I couldn't sit all the way back in the chair. I sat on the very edge, frozen from head to toe. I needed to do something to get my mind off that encounter with the teacher and how nervous I was. I reached into a folder I had brought to look at something special I had taken with me that day.

It was a Cuban magazine that included a cover story about my dad's work in rural Cuba. My maternal grandma had sent it to me. The paper was yellowish brown, and she had preserved the fragile pages with a long strip of tape along the spine. It was too dark in the auditorium to read, but there was enough light to see my dad's pure smile. I was very proud to be his daughter and was amazed at how much he had accomplished from the time that magazine had been published to that moment in spring of 2018. My eyes got really watery for a second. I showed some friends the magazine and that helped me breathe a little. I said, "This my dad. He was a doctor in Cuba." One of them mentioned that he looked like an actor. I laughed because several people have said that he looks like Benicio del Toro from the Heineken commercial.

When I was called up to one of the tables on the stage I was still freezing. But when I began talking and moving my hands all over the place to explain all the questions, I felt warm and much more confident. I was surprised that I didn't stumble on my words.

I was myself during the interview, and that that was enough, along with my resume, to get me into the pre-med magnet, my first step to becoming a doctor.

Surprised and content, I felt a relief when I found out my acceptance. When I told my parents the news, my dad advised, "Meli, this is just the beginning. These essentials will give you a great base for the future. Pay close attention." Mom and Dad gave me a tight hug and said,

"Esa es nuestra niña, estamos muy orgullosos de ti. Eres una fiera."

That's our girl. We're so proud of you. You are fierce.

SYLVIA
D. LONTZ

THE STARS WILL WHISPER BACK

We are jolted out of our innocence once we realize what the world truly is. It's an abrupt realization when we learn the tooth fairy isn't putting money under our pillows at night: it's our parents pulling enough change together to make us smile in the morning. We realize a bunny isn't the one filling up our Easter baskets and leaving eggs in the front yard: it's our family who got the Great Value pack of Easter eggs from the Dollar Tree and told us not to look out the window as they spread the eggs around. We discover the jolly white man isn't the one putting presents under the Christmas tree: it's people from the church and the community who were generous enough to give poor kids what they wanted, and our parents who tried to help out as much as possible.

As a kid, you see living in a motel room as an adventure. You see an abusive husband as a confused man. You see a visit to the jail as a field trip with your mom. You don't see times like these as rough times. I never looked at my surroundings and saw the bad things about them, even though there was always some more bad news around the corner. I didn't realize how messed up my childhood really was until I grew up. The chaotic parts of my life came from moving around and switching schools every few years, trying to make new friends and adjust to the new world we found ourselves in, yet again. The chaos also came from living in a house with a single mother and four sisters.

The man who made me was never around. He never even laid eyes on my face. I never got to run in the front door after school and say, "Hey Dad!" and tell him how my day went, or listen to stories about how hard he worked that day, or what adventures he and my mother had together. He didn't care about me, didn't claim me, didn't even admit that he had a daughter. I never have known what he looks like, how he smells, what it feels like to hug him or be held in his arms. I never got to buy a Father's Day card, and I couldn't relate to the kids in kindergarten who talked about how strong their dads were, or how much their parents loved each other.

My earliest memories are in a little country town called Leitchfield, Kentucky. Things were much different than they are now. It was just me and my older sister, Kayla. We lived in a nice neighborhood full of small houses and quiet families. I only remember a few summers and springs there, but I'm amazed at how many memories my mind developed as a child that I can still recall.

In the small living room, we had a huge box television on the floor with a game console on top of it. The kitchen was painted a light sky-blue color, and I spent hours jumping up and down in a bouncy swing that hung in the doorway. I once burned my hand on a toaster in that little kitchen. I recall the little teal seat I would sit on in the bathtub when I was a little baby. The back door led to a big open field where I played with my neighbor Gracie. She was a

little white girl like me, but with big blue eyes. I went to preschool and kindergarten with her, and we swore to each other that we would always be best friends as we bonded on her trampoline. But now I don't even know where she is. It's funny how many people come and go in life but whose memory sticks with you along the way.

I still think of my first crush in kindergarten, a little Mexican boy with cute dimples and long eyelashes. I remember going to school for the first time, and I reminisce about the time Kayla hid me under a jacket in the back of the bus so I could sit with her and her friend. The rules said that I was too little to sit in the back of the bus, but Kayla always stuck with me no matter what anyone said. That's just how it was when we were younger.

Those four years still remain very clear in my mind. But all of that came to an abrupt end when my mom divorced my newborn sister Spheara's dad. I had just turned five, and everything we had built our lives on was thrown to the curb. The memories of her father and his family filled the neighborhood I grew up in. We just had to get away, so we abandoned it all, and my childhood was over: four years of dirt bike rides, of jumping off of Red Rock into the lake where we spent our summers, four years in a small town elementary school, of my church where I dreaded old ladies telling me how cute I was and squeezing my cheeks until they turned pink, four years of playing with worms and acting like pilgrims in my cousin's big backyard, of cookouts and tree houses, of rolling down enormous grassy hills, of falling asleep on soft carpets in front of the fireplace at my aunt and uncle's house, four years of playing in the rain, of pitch black nights lying on the grass counting the stars, which was one of the most memorable things about that place.

I still think of those stars all the time—so bright and so far away, but seemingly just in my reach, like I could hold them in my hands, protect them, keep them safely locked up in a secret place, like they could give off heat in the palm of our hands. When we're kids, we wish on them, we tell our secrets to them so quietly in the dark, and they hear us speaking softly when we say, *Amen.* If you listen closely, you can hear them, whispering back. They can tell you your fortune, your future, your destiny.

I still hold Leitchfield and those stars close to my heart. I didn't get the chance to stay in one place again for years and years. I didn't have a home that I can pinpoint in my mind. I know that we stayed with my aunt for a while. And I remember staying with a sweet old woman we called Ms.Susie who took my mother under her wing when we had no one else to turn to. I called her Grandma and she taught us Spanish numbers and helped us put a bunk bed together. She was the only person my mother trusted for a while, the only friend my mother had. She was an amazing person, a good Christian lady who only meant well. For a while we lived in a beat up old trailer park with a small kitchen and even smaller rooms. I remember holding my newborn baby sister Aleila for the first time there. I remember a crack addict banging on our door at three o'clock in the morning demanding drugs. I remember the pretty bathtub and the glowing stars Kayla put on her ceiling.

Some time later, we found a more permanent, more independent spot across from the church that provided it for us. The people from the church

called it The Oasis House, and it became our oasis, our fertile spot in a chaotic world. A place in the middle of the desert in which we were lost where we could produce hope, grow as a family. A place we could finally call home. It was a small brick house off the side of a main road, hidden by the trees growing around it. A small place that went unnoticed by most. We spent one summer and one Christmas there. I have a few memories of catching lizards in the yard and riding around on my scooter in the driveway during the summer and building a fort in my bedroom out of blankets and pillows. I remember my mother telling us she was pregnant with my youngest sister Niya as we sat around our small kitchen table. Then one day we suddenly packed our whole lives up in boxes and left this place where I'd felt I could be a kid again.

Once the church kicked us out of this so-called oasis, we were lost with nowhere to go once again. It wasn't the first time I experienced disappointment and abandonment, and I knew it wouldn't be the last. I was becoming used to the feeling. I remember the pained expression that developed on my mother's face as a result of it. The look wasn't angry, but sad and hopeless. There was an on-edge feeling that settled among my family for what was to come.

We stayed at a Motel 6 next to a gas station just off an exit in Shepherdsville. Thousands of cars passed every day without noticing the motel. It was nothing but a pit stop for late night drivers and travelers. All of our belongings were stuffed into garbage bags in our small room. We slept on bed sheets burnt by cigarette butts. The four walls that closed us in from the outside world were the only four walls we could afford at the time, and it was home for a short time.

But as a kid, I never looked at my surroundings and saw the bad things about them. I woke up one morning in that hotel happy as I could be in a bed I was convinced was my own. A huge smile spread across my face the moment I woke up; I was turning seven that day.

"Mom, today's gonna be so fun!" I exclaimed as she rose out of the bed next to mine. Her socks touched the filthy floor and she asked, "Why, what's going on today?" as if she was clueless.

"It's my birthday!"

"What!? No!" She said sarcastically as she giggled and picked me up and swung me around. I grabbed some clothes out of a garbage bag and threw them on. My mom placed a pink Birthday Girl pin onto my shirt. I looked with joy in the dirty mirror at my small innocent face and the three dollars she stuck behind the pin. It wasn't much, but it was enough. It always was.

Mom smiled to cover up her pained expression like she always did. It's a face only the strongest people could learn to cover up. The forced smiles and beautiful worry lines that form over years of pain from a broken family, abusive relationships, unaccepting parents, from the ashes of drug addicts. My mother is the strongest person I know, and I have always wanted to be like her, even though she tells me she wants me to be better than her. I hope one day I'll be as strong as she is. She's always had a spark in her. She's a great poet and writer. She has a wild look in her eyes when she's creating something. She never cares what anyone thinks and does not mind embarrassing you or herself in public. I guess that's a mother thing.

I know she would risk everything for me, and she always has my back no matter what. In negative situations she is always positive and keeps a smile on her face to protect her children. The sky could be falling outside with my mother watching, and I wouldn't be able to tell because I would look at her and see nothing but a comforting smile and bright wild eyes. She has always protected me and my siblings against the bad things in the world.

One time when we were living in The Oasis House, we were under a tornado watch. We all had to get in the bathtub as the thunder and lightning screamed so loudly outside you could feel it in your bones. My sisters and I were terrified and thought that our house was going to tumble down around us and possibly take us with it. As we all huddled together in the tiny bathtub, I looked up at my mother. She had a stern, serious look on her face. She simply said, "Everything's going to be fine. There's nothing to worry about. We just have to be safe." And with that, we all felt safe again.

I think it's a superpower that my mom has. Whether I'm looking at my grandma in a casket, staring at the blood gushing out of my knee after falling down outside, losing faith on the sidelines as we are about to lose at a basketball game, or feeling nervous when things get a little shaky as my teammates on the cheerleading team are lifting me into the air, with a simple look she can mend any pain. The thing about having a mom like mine is you can always look for her and just know she'll be there, cheering you on, offering a shoulder to cry on if necessary, standing there with open arms always. In the worst of storms, I can look over my shoulder and know that she'll be there no matter what.

There was a park in Shepherdsville where my mom would take us and a long trail there where I took one of my first bike rides. There was a river that ran all the way through on the edge of the park, and on peaceful days you could hear the rush of the water dancing hand in hand with the wind. We spent many hot days running around in the open fields and up and down that trail. In the spring when it rained too much, the river would flood, engulfing the track and some of the field. My mother warned us away from the edge, saying we would get pulled in and taken away by the water if we got too close. The days the park was flooded the water would sit still in an eerie way and there would only be movement caused by unidentified objects every so often.

One day in the beginning of April, when I was eleven years old, Spheara was seven, Aleila was

four, and Niya was three, (Kayla was sixteen but was spending the day with a friend), we walked along the trail for a while in the opposite direction of what we usually took. The sky was blue and clear that day and the colors reminded me of stained glass. It felt perfect as the sun kissed our skin. The breeze caught my hair and sent chills up my spine, giving me goosebumps. We discovered a baseball field that had gone unnoticed to us until that day. Behind the field was a huge hill. My sisters and I still had energy, so my mom made us race.

My legs were numb and my heart raced, but I didn't stop until my body wanted to give out. I struggled to catch my breath as I pushed my body further. The adrenaline rush came from the feeling of almost falling when I went down the hill. The thought of slipping didn't even touch my mind. I

was immune to doubt and fear. That's the funny thing about being a kid: you never really think things can go wrong, and if you do, you almost automatically dismiss it. You're immune to the fear of falling, the fear of being abandoned, the fear of losing someone or getting lost, the fear of getting hurt or judged. As a child, you simply don't care; the worries that follow you as a teenager and adult just haven't developed in your mind yet. To a young child, this is blissful and normal.

Once we were finally tired, we sat down on some stairs. My mother pulled out her outdated flip phone to capture the moment. We smiled from ear to ear at the camera as we caught our breath. After that, we raced back to the car and got on the road. The wind blew throughout the entire beat-up minivan as my sisters and I yelled out the words to the radio hits from the summer of 2015: Justin Bieber, Britney Spears, Miley Cyrus. The sun still cast its liquid gold rays on the world around me.

As it started to get dark, the music and people grew quiet. We weren't back in the city yet, and I admired the beauty of the stars as the moonlight shone on my face. I tried to convince myself it would always be like this: peaceful, perfect, blissful. As I got older, nights and days like these became scarce. But that day, I thought the world was perfect. A world where nothing went wrong.

There was another person who came into our life during a lot of these years of moving around. My mom had started dating a guy back when I was about five years old. I vaguely remember my first encounter with him. It was when we were living with my aunt, and I was sitting on the kitchen floor playing with some toys when my mother came through the front door with a man I had never seen before. He was tall and skinny and had brown skin, no hair, and brown eyes. His voice was deep and intimidating. He moved in a swift and abrupt way. When he saw me, our eyes met and a smile formed on his face. I stumbled to my feet, looking at my mom standing beside him. I expected her to say he was a maintenance man or someone coming to help with the house, but then she looked at my sisters and I and said four simple words that changed my life: "Girls, this is Lamont." Initially I was confused. I didn't know if they were friends or acquaintances or partners.

"So is that, like, your boyfriend?" I spoke of him as if he was an object, not knowing how to put it. My mother looked at me as if I had just asked her what color clouds are. "Um, yeah? What did you think he was?"

So with that, this new man entered our lives. At first I didn't know how to approach him. It took a long time to get used to seeing him around the house, and it was weird to see my mother spend time with a man and show affection to him. It was something I hadn't seen in a long time. But I began to notice that my mom was smiling more and laughing more. She had always been bubbly and positive, but now she had a new glow to her.

It took me a while to trust that he wouldn't leave or change up like everything else in my life, but after he was around for about a year I started to get comfortable, and the weight on my shoulders began to lift. I remember one of the first Christmases we all spent together after he'd been with Mom for a while. He stood beside my mom as he watched all of us opening our presents with the biggest smile on his face.

He looked like the proudest man. It seemed like he would actually stick around for the coming Christmases and Thanksgivings. In the midst of celebrating holidays and developing good memories that would forever be engraved in my mind, my sisters Aleila and Niya were born. My mother became pregnant with my sister Aleila when we were living in the trailer. About a year after that, when we were living in The Oasis House, Niya was born. With two new siblings in my life, my days were beginning to reshape themselves. My mom was so happy and so were my sisters. Lamont had three sons as well—Myron, Cameron and Thomas—who I began to consider my brothers, and we have all become one huge, crazy, loud, and loving family.

The word "step" began to fall away from "dad" and "brothers." Forget DNA and the technicalities of biology: Lamont is mine. He is my dad. I'm glad I have someone in my life who takes responsibility for his actions and actually takes care of his kids and their family. I believe that's what it means to be a man. It takes courage.

He always manages to make me smile, just like he does with everyone else. He doesn't even have to put any effort towards it. He has the ability to brighten anyone's day. He has a free spirit and never cares what people think about him. He can be very laid back but also hyper and goofy. He is the only person I know that can make you laugh when you're crying. Like this one time, we were sitting in the parking lot of Walgreens Pharmacy. It was springtime, the air was cool and the wind steady. A song came on that my dad loved, and he immediately started dancing and yelling out the words. There was an old white couple in the car next to us. They seemed surprised and a little scared. Lamont looked over at them and still didn't miss a beat. He couldn't care less if people were looking. He was fearless in the pursuit of his goofiness.

He loves my mother unconditionally, and that's what I love most about him. My parents have been together for twelve years now, and their relationship has become a beautiful one. I hope I can find something like theirs when I'm older. He is just what my mom needed, and he came into her life at the perfect time.

By the time I was nine or ten years old, we'd been kicked out, let down, and had moved from place to place. "Home" was a distant idea of something that only other people had. Then my mom heard about a place in downtown Louisville that was building brand new apartments. It was being paid for through a shelter called The Center for Women and Families which was across from where the apartments were being built. She called the shelter every day asking when they would be available. They told her hundreds of times that our family was too big, that there wasn't enough room, that we wouldn't fit, but still my mother called and called and called. Every single day she got the same answer. But eventually, we were able to live there, and we finally had the chance to settle down somewhere in a space we could call our own.

My dad began living with us when we moved into this new place. I felt the same about him as I did the new house: still a little unsure. I didn't think either one would be permanent, so I tried not to take these new changes seriously. I knew if I got my hopes

up, I might get let down again. It was hard not to think that we would end up leaving this place just like all the others. After a few months, though, I slowly started to believe it would be permanent. Once we settled down and I could finally trust that we were going to be there for a while, I grew up a lot in that apartment. We were there for ten years. It was small for our big family, but we managed to make it work and learned how to tolerate it. When I look in each of the rooms in that apartment, about a million flashbacks and memories go through my head. Each room has a different story.

So many Thanksgivings happened at our table in that small cluttered kitchen. So many Christmases spent in that kitchen baking and decorating dozens of cookies at once. So many big meals and family gatherings. I would climb on the counters to reach

Whatever we had, wherever we were, I knew everything was going to be okay.

the cereal that was on top of the fridge and the shelf where the bowls were stored. The two bookshelves looked as though they would swallow the huge kitchen table next to them. The hundreds of books on the shelves made it seem even more cluttered. But that was only the kitchen.

Downstairs between the living room and the kitchen was a small bathroom. I got my hair cut for the first time in that bathroom. I got ready every morning for school in that bathroom all throughout middle school. And, years later, I started my period in that bathroom.

In my mother's room, there were a hundred mornings when I would sit on the floor next to her bed as she fixed my hair. I would come to her room at night and sit on her bed just to talk when I couldn't sleep. I would sweep the stairs when I was trying to be an obedient child. When I would hear my mother's voice echo as she called my name from downstairs, I would groan, knowing I would have to do some type of favor or chore. I had my first sleepover in that living room, and I learned how to do a handstand and a cartwheel there. I would practice my cheers countless times in that living room after making the cheerleading team in eighth grade. The middle room upstairs was originally mine before my older sister Kayla moved out. It was the tiniest room. We called

it "the little box"; it was the most cramped room out of the three. It had a bunk bed, a dresser, a toy kitchen my sisters played with, a TV, and a shelf. My sisters and I had so many sleepovers, concerts and dance battles in that tiny room. I would bring my first best friend in that room and we would spill out our secrets to each other on the top bunk, which was my bed.

We would play outside for hours and hours in the endless summers. When snow filled the ground, we built plenty of snowmen. One summer I saved my money up and had about forty dollars. We went to a sports equipment store and that's where I found them: pearly white skates with purple wheels and a logo that said Roller Derby. They immediately caught my eye. When I got them home, all the kids around the neighborhood stopped in astonishment when I glided swiftly down the sidewalk. Moments like those are what stick out in my mind when I think about our time living there.

We were there for ten years and we were happy inside our tiny, cluttered home, but I think we picked that place not because we wanted to, but because we had to. We didn't really have a lot of options. To the right of us there was a nice Mexican family that was always peaceful and quiet, but we also lived next to some people who hadn't grown up in the best circumstances. There was a woman who lived next to us who had so much junk in her apartment that she gave us roaches at one point. Upstairs were the worst neighbors. We weren't allowed to go up there.

One night, after we had been living there for a few years, I was lying in my bed looking into the darkness. I was just about to drift off into sleep when I heard something above me that sounded as if it was going to come through the ceiling and fall onto my head. It was a loud bang and I knew someone was throwing things, furniture maybe. I could hear doors slamming. I heard them yelling things like "Where's the money?" and "What did you do with it?" The other voice sounded scared rather than angry: "Chill out, bruh. Calm down." There was one final slam of a door that rattled my whole room and then nothing but silence fell over me after. Who knows what they were arguing about. I looked at my ceiling as the darkness and silence fell around me. I drifted off to sleep and escaped into my dreams, where things were simpler and more peaceful. This was where the bad things went away. But some nights I couldn't sleep because there would be so much going on in life that I couldn't convince myself to fall asleep.

There were rumors that another woman who lived next to us was a prostitute. A different man would go into her house every few days and leave at odd hours of the night. She would send her daughter outside while she was "getting things done" and force her to play with the other kids in the neighborhood, which sometimes included my sisters and me. Her daughter was completely oblivious to what her mother was doing all day. She would say the men were her friends or called a few of them her boyfriend. My mother told us it was none of our business and to stay out of it.

I often felt bad for that little girl. She was almost never in the house, forced outside no matter if there was a heat wave or five inches of snow on the ground. She always asked us for water and food, and we gave it to her when we could. My sisters seemed to enjoy her company. They often played together and their voices would collide as they began giggling loudly and yelling. I knew the people I lived next to came from

not so ideal circumstances, but I also knew there was hope for them just like everyone else. Hope for them to change and hope for them to create a better life.

I always felt as though I had enough. To others, what I had probably didn't look like much. But to me, if I had my parents and sisters to turn to, I was okay. That was all I needed. They didn't even have to say anything. A simple glance from my mom or a smile from Kayla or a laugh from Spheara was enough. Whatever we had, wherever we were, I knew everything was going to be okay.

When you are growing up, moving from place to place all the time, when you become used to a forever changing environment, it's embedded in your brain that that's how it's always going to be and that's how

it's supposed to be. When you're moving around all the time, when your friends are changing, your house is changing, your circumstances are changing, it's not necessarily healthy. You kind of detach yourself from the words "home" and "stability." But when you're given the opportunity to live in the same place for a while, when you are in a stable home, it gives you hope and faith.

There's constant chaos in our family. But occasionally there's also the strong smell of cookies from our tiny cluttered kitchen that touches you from all the way upstairs. Smiles form on all of our faces when we gather around the table and discuss life and things beyond it. I've peeked at my mother sitting at the end of the table to find tears sliding quietly down her cheeks as she managed to say a prayer. When I was young, I never understood why she would cry during

happy moments. Once I got older, I started to understand that they weren't tears of pain, but tears of happiness that came from emotion built up within her. It came from staying strong all year for her family and holding all the emotions back, never breaking down. At times like these she was reminded of how blessed we were to make it through another year.

Somehow we always ended up at that table filled with food and the faces of my family, crying, praying and laughing together. That small, cluttered, place filled with the smell of cookies, brownies, apple cider, ham, and turkey, the place where we could escape to for sanctuary. The place where the outside world was nothing but a blur of bad things that could be ignored while we were all finally at peace with ourselves and the world around us.

I know a lot of people have more than me, but I also know a lot of people have less than me. Ultimately I am thankful for the things I have and the family I am given. No matter where I am, no matter where I go, I have learned what home is and where to find it. When I was younger, I began to believe home was a place. I started to believe this because I was moving around so much, looking for what I thought was a home. But then I began to realize as I got a little older that I had a home all along, no matter where I was. I have learned that home can be found in someone and not somewhere.

Throughout my high school experience, I've gone through a lot of ups and downs, like any teenager. Some things sent me into a spiral of confusion and self-doubt. At times I've been a weak mirror that was suddenly shattered when my thoughts became dangerous to my self-esteem. In the middle of my mental instability, a place formed in my mind where there was a beautiful yard filled with exquisite roses. I somehow got up the courage to keep plunging deeper into the garden, to continue to explore myself and face the challenges life threw at me. My family became my rose of reassurance. They put me back together when I was broken and showed me the light in darkness.

Because of them, I have become thankful for everything. I realize how precious the little things are; having people that love and support me. They all have opened my eyes to see the beauty of overcoming a shattered past and coming from a broken home. I've reflected on my life and noticed how blessed I am to have a roof over my head, food on my plate for dinner, and a loving family.

And I've realized who I really am: a goofy, loud, smart, dramatic, poetic, weird mess who's filled with bright and dark colors. I am a multi-dimensional, incredible being. I've learned to embrace every aspect of my life, good and bad, the perfect imperfections, negative and positive, happy and sad, through the ups and downs, hardships and good times. I embrace and love every single moment and every part of myself: little and big, perfect and imperfect.

PHOTO BY

NATALIA
UNSELD

BOUND NOT BY BLOOD

When I was four years old, I first saw the man who would eventually become my dad. I heard him and my mom laughing, so I peeked on the other side of the wall in our basement to see if I could recognize this stranger. He was sitting on the brown leather couch with his feet crossed upon the footstool. He and my mom exchanged smiles. The basement's shivering cold air made goosebumps appear on my arms and legs. I didn't mind, though. I was too busy staring at him. The only things I could focus on were his white pearly teeth and the smell of his cologne. My mom introduced us, informing me she'd been seeing him for a while and that she thought it would be a good time for the two of us to meet. The only thing my four-year-old mind comprehended was, "This is Mommy's boyfriend." I didn't know what to say or think. I went mute. "Go ahead, introduce yourself," Mom said. I introduced myself and surprised myself by shaking his hand. "Hi, I am Daryle," he said. "Nice to meet you."

After that day this stranger—who I started to call Mr. Daryle—came over very often. We started to form a friendship with one another, a close connection, a bond. I thought of him as my friend instead of "Mommy's boyfriend." I waited every night for him to come over for dinner. The sound of the doorbell ringing made the hairs on my neck stand up, in a good way. My mom would get up from the kitchen table to welcome him in and I would always follow her to greet him with the world's strongest hug. The second I turned the corner our eyes would lock, exchanging a mutual feeling of excitement. I would run up to him and he'd pick me up and spin me around with a wide smile on his face, stretching from ear to ear.

I didn't quite understand just yet the impact of my biological father not being in my life. But when I went to my other friends' houses and was greeted by both of their parents, I felt like I was being left out, like I couldn't relate. Even at such a young age, I could sense that my life didn't match the lives of those around me. I was envious of the genial smiles of the "complete" families taking family walks in the neighborhood or making short trips to the grocery store together. I felt a growing ball of frustration while seeing other families enjoying their time together and creating memories.

At that point, it was just me and my mom. She had me and I had her. We had each other. I depended on her for just about everything. It was clear that I only had one parent. I never knew what a "deadbeat father" was. I didn't even know there was a title for that. I just knew how horrible I felt after a long day of waiting for him to potentially arrive at my house to pick me up for an outing we had planned. I always knew my mom would do anything to make my pain go away. At times she stressed herself out more than I stressed, so I decided to keep my feelings to myself.

I didn't even realize it, but I established a routine for myself when I came home from school. I'd drop my bag off and would immediately shift my attention over to the tiny table next to the couch. That table held the house phone and thus the possibility of speaking with my father. As I approached it, I felt a rush of adrenaline begin to rise into me, starting in my feet and warmly maneuvering its way through the pit of my stomach.

Time after time I would call and call his phone only to get sent back to square one. *Ring, ring, ring… You've been sent to the automatic voicemail box of 502….* The voicemail again and again. Ring ring, ring ring ring, *You've been sent to the automatic voicemail of…* This would go on so long I'd lose track of time. All I wanted to hear was the click of him picking up from the other end of the phone. The click that meant acceptance. I wanted to hear his voice say something, anything. Just simply, "Hey, I want to get to know you better." I hated the phone for replaying the same automatic message. He couldn't come to the phone.

When he did answer, our conversation would go a little something like this. "H-hey dad," I would say. "Hey, Bink! What are you doing?" I'd respond with a

"nothing much," when in all realness I wanted to say, *I've been waiting for your call for days now.* A nonstop train of curious thoughts would run in and out of my head for days, maybe even weeks, and the only thing I received from him was "Hey, what's up?" as if he'd talked to me the day before. But I was still so stoked to even get an answer from him.

Sometimes we'd make plans to spend time together, and sometimes he actually followed through with those plans. One time when I was eight years old, my mom drove me all the way to the mall just to meet up with him. Though it had been a long time since I had seen him, I spotted him immediately. As soon as I stepped out of the car I bolted towards him. My braided pigtails with my barrettes swayed back and forth in the harsh yet soft wind. I ran into his arms and he lifted me what felt like ten feet into the air. We embraced each other strongly. Being in his presence wrapped me in a thick, cozy blanket of security.

I loved all the times when he actually followed through with our plans, and I wished those moments could last forever. But then he would leave me for days, weeks, and sometimes months without a trace of where he went.

"I promise I'll pick you up on Wednesday at three. I promise, babe!" I would agree with just about anything he told me because him calling me back to make false plans felt better than not hearing from him at all. I sat and waited and waited and waited on that Wednesday at three o'clock. I kept looking back and forth at the clock, saying to myself, *He'll be here in about five minutes. It shouldn't take him long.* Each time the clock would meet my time, I gave him more excuses for being extremely late.

Being surrounded by supportive compassion during times like this always made things a little better.

When night time came I was so confused that even crying didn't feel like the right thing to do. His absence left me to sit up at night thinking, *Is it something I did?*

There were so many broken promises, yet I continued to run back and call him, knowing without a doubt that he wouldn't answer. He has always had a soft spot in my heart. He is the reason I am here today. I spent so much time waiting that I even created a mini notebook to fill with memories of just him and me together. I knew a lot of my friends had their fathers in their lives and talked about the memories they'd had together. I was never really able to relate, so this notebook was my way of feeling like I could relate. I planned to save it as I got older, but unfortunately, there was never anything to put inside of it.

I began blaming everything and everyone except for the person who deserved the most blame for the entirety of this situation. I was a child trying to defend the man I called my father even though he would leave me to count the cars that would pass until he showed. "Mom, I don't know what to do. I am so confused I don't know what to feel." This is a sample of 99.9% of how our conversations would go. "It's okay to feel confused." She would always be the one to take the blindfold off and remind me that a

person who really loves you would never leave you to guess for days about where they are. They would keep in contact with you and regularly check in with you. I can still just look at my mom and see straight through her heart: she would literally save my life over hers. She would do anything at any cost to protect her family. Since I was her only child she paid close attention to the things she knew affected me.

Being surrounded by supportive compassion during times like this always made things a little better. But my mom couldn't take away the endless train of dark thoughts that circled in my head at night, constant reminders of what I didn't have in my life.

Looking back to eight-year-old Natalia, she felt like she needed closure. If not that, at least a "Hey, just wanted to check in on you." I was searching for an explanation as to how you could ever do this to someone you claim you love, yet show no remorse for your actions. I have learned from my mom that nine times out of ten people do what's best for them, and sometimes those people are your own family members.

As I matured, the calls from my end started coming less and less frequently. It took me to stop calling him for him to start calling me. That's when it clicked for me: I had never been the problem. I no longer wait for the call that holds my worth, my acceptance, or my time. Now the script is flipped. Now *he* calls to say, "Hey, I was just seeing how you're doing, you know it feels like we haven't talked in forever."

Once Mr. Daryle came into my life, it was easier to just brush it off and pretend it didn't bother me because at least I had somebody who was there to replace his spot. At this point in my life, I am very comfortable with the fact that my biological dad is not in the picture due to my dad now filling in his spot. I have learned to accept the wrong in my life. I have grown to understand we can't choose who our family is, nor does that automatically make them do right by you at all costs. I have learned it's okay not to be okay.

Although my biological father was out of the picture, I was constantly surrounded by adults and older family members who I knew had my back regardless. At Sunday gatherings with my family, just seeing all of their smiling faces while the barbecue aroma lingered in the air instantly gave me a warm, tender feeling. We would all sit around and eat, while my five uncles and two aunts told the same old stories from their childhood and we listened to, as they would call it, "feel-good music" by groups like Maze—the type of music that brought families and communities together to forget about their problems and just kick back, relax, and dance. The adults played cards while swatting flies away from their faces. My cousins Ben and Alex and I recklessly ran around chasing each other, playing tag for the tenth time in a row. I remember getting nervous to go across the monkey bars as my cousins threatened to pull me down if I didn't hurry up. "Don't be horse playing too much, you don't wanna mess up your pretty hair," my grandma would always remind me. As a kid, even the little positive affirmations from family members allowed me to realize that not all of my family is tied to a negative association in my life. I was surrounded by those who I loved and those who loved me. Though I didn't realize it at the time, moments like this are the reason why family has always meant the most to me.

After two years together, my mom and Mr. Daryle got engaged. This was when I met Jasmyne, my soon-to-be-stepsister. I was five and she was thirteen. I had always fantasized about the sister-sister relationships I had seen on TV. My first encounter with Jasmyne was cordial. Soon our cordialness quickly transformed into mutual hatred. We fought constantly. She would accuse me of losing the cap off the toothpaste or stealing her lip gloss. To her, I was an annoying little kid. To me, this was the sister I'd always wanted, someone I could look up to besides my parents. In a way, I purposely wanted to make her mad at me, just to laugh and to argue for fun. I knew this was what sisters were supposed to do.

They say they don't remember me being there, but I remember every second of the moment my parents got engaged. It was a school night, and my mom had just cooked my favorite meal for my dad and me. I excused myself from the table to go to the bathroom. Just as I was finishing drying off my hands I heard, "OH MY GOSH!" followed by a loud, never-ending scream. I peeked my head around the corner, making sure I stayed hidden. Though no one had ever sat me down and explained to me what the next step meant for two people who were truly in love, I had observed from the movies my mom and I would spend hours binge-watching and had overheard my grandparents talk on and on about how they met. I knew what came next. As I peeked my head around the corner, I saw her hold the phone with a smile that stretched ear to ear. I knew that her best friend was on the other end of the line. I wish I had been able to see my dad on one knee exchanging a smile with my mom, both frozen in time, looking into each other's eyes. I wish I had been there to see my dad anticipating my mom's response.

Shortly after they got engaged, my parents told me and Jasmyne that we'd be going to Florida for a family vacation. I believe it was strategically structured for all four of us to bond more closely. What I thought was a trip they pulled out of thin air to surprise my sister and me was actually a trip that took several months of planning.

The trip started off on the wrong foot as soon as we stepped inside the airport. A rush of cold air blew right over me and I was blinded by the dazzling lights that reflect off of the glistening pale white floor. We headed over to the line to drop off our luggage. I leaned over to hug my dad and said, "Daddy, I am so excited!" The sentence was barely complete when Jasmyne said, "Daddy? He's my dad, not yours!"

I was so confused. I couldn't grasp why she snapped at me. I snapped back so quickly that I couldn't keep up with my own words. "No, he's mine!"

"Hey hey, hey!!" our parents said in sync. They both gave Jasmyne the infamous adult eye.

This was going to be my potential sister. Us calling the same person "Dad" shouldn't spark conflict. If anything, I thought it should draw us closer. After things wound back down, I could still feel the burning rage lingering with a slight blaze to it. I clung to Dad.

At the time, Jasmyne hadn't fully adjusted to the fact that we were basically sisters. I expected those around me, Jasmyne in particular, to feel the same way about becoming siblings and sharing the same dad. I never considered Jasmyne's side of the story. After all, she was already seeing him off and on in her relationship. She came over every summer for at least a month and stayed for other school breaks, but she lived with her mom and her stepdad.

Due to growing up an only child I never really considered the other side and how people may differ from me. I was still pretty self-involved and oblivious to most things around me.

It was a long, horrendous day of traveling, and the airplane ride to Florida was viciously bumpy. As we rode the bus to the baggage claim, I fell over in my seat next to Jasmyne out of pure exhaustion. I felt a gentle hand lean my head over into her lap. As tired as I was, I couldn't infer whether this gesture meant she was done being mad at me or she wanted to get the snoring out of her ear. I lay there pretending to sleep as I grinned widely in my head. *She's showing me attention now, she must actually like me now*, I thought to myself.

Little did I know this was going to be one of the hundred times our moods would switch just within a short time fragment. As Jasmyne and I left one of the Disney World Halloween celebration parties with our parents, I thought everything was going smoothly when she snapped, "Natalia, will you just shut up!" I snapped back, "Since when are you in charge to tell me to shut up! Don't talk to me like that!" My mom told me to get onto the bus back to the hotel and stop holding up the people behind us. Being dramatic, I stopped dead in front of the bus with my scrunched eyebrows and glossy eyes staring directly at Jasmyne. The next day we went right back to how things were as if nothing happened. She did my hair for me right before we went anywhere on the Disney trip, asking, "Is it too high? If you don't like it, I can always change it." And she cared enough to outfit check me before we left to go anywhere on this trip. She'd say, "If I were you I'd choose the pink bow. It goes better with your shirt." Though it felt like she always was shooing

me away, at the same time it felt like we were growing closer together as actual sisters.

Everything just had to be peaches and cream for my mom's wedding. The wedding rehearsals at the church were directed by Mrs. Williams, the wedding planner. She was a woman of her word who you wouldn't dare cross. Whatever she says goes. She never messed around when it came to her clients. She made my mom and I feel like we were the only things that mattered. We practiced non-stop at the church. Despite the worn-out faces among the others who were participating in the wedding, I never showed signs of being tired. I knew what this meant for my mom and refused to embarrass her on her big day. I made sure to smile every time I went down the aisle, even if it was for practice. I am sure I could do the same walk I practiced five hundred times for the wedding till this day.

It was late afternoon and all of the women stood around in the dressing room waiting for the next clue on where to go next while my cousins and I ran around the halls of the church, regardless of all the disappointed glances from the adults around us. It sounded like an old family reuniting over small talk. Phrases like "He's gotten so big!" echoed off of the walls of the church. My cousins and I ran around aimlessly through the outraged voices of adults saying, "You're going to ruin your outfits! Stop running before you hurt yourselves!" I had one more time to bump into a stranger's leg with a *sorry, scuse me* until I ran right into my uncle's leg. I was mad that I ended up getting tagged, but I knew it was better for him to catch us running around like this instead of Mrs. Williams.

I could just imagine the infamous fierce adult eye every kid would experience right before getting into serious trouble.

I headed back into the dressing room. It was full of bridesmaids zipping up each other's dresses. My grandma and mom sat in the corner going back and forth debating the fact that my grandma crying was making my mom cry. "NO, you must not cry, You'll mess up your makeup!" my grandma insisted.

In the midst of all of the chaos, I stood in the mirror and continued to practice my commercial smile and my picture-perfect posture as I imagined myself walking down the aisle until Ms. Williams opened the door. She smiled as her stray hairs dangled out of her neatly pinned updo. I knew her smile was forced due to all of the chaos around us.

All of the bridesmaids made their way down the aisle one after another. Finally, it was my turn. I linked arms with my cousin DJ and nervously began to walk. I couldn't help but notice the stares from all the way in front of the church. The church was filled with the aunts and uncles I would only see during Christmas. The church had tall ceilings with brown wooden arches with fans the pastor swore worked, but hadn't worked in years. I saw my dad's face, which instantly put a smile on my face. I walked to the front of the altar and stood next to my sister in front of the bridesmaids.

I couldn't wait to see my mom walk down the aisle in the dress I knew she loved so dearly. It was intimidating to stand in the front being analyzed and observed by everyone in the church, but the choir stood and began to sing a soft melody that put me at ease.

The piano then shifted gears to the famous wedding song that plays in the movies every time the brides walk down the aisle. Now it all started feeling like a dream. Ever since Mom got engaged she had started binge-watching *Say Yes to the Dress* daily. At the rate she watched it, it couldn't have been healthy. Every Friday night we cuddled up on the living room couch with the lights off and glued our eyes to the TV as soon as that show came on. Though I had no clue what was going on, I watched anyway. I just loved the quality time we spent with each other, especially during this time, while we both anticipated such a huge moment for her. It felt surreal to think my mom would be one of those famous TV women in the gleaming white dresses with pearly whites and the fancy updos that made you question how long it took to do them.

The doors swung open and revealed a beautiful bride I could barely even recognize. She was supposedly the same person who tucked me in at night and walked around in her house sweats and nerd glasses at home. She cuffed arms with my grandad and they made their way down the aisle. I knew my grandfather well enough to know his "I am feeling hesitant" face. I knew he approved of my dad, but this time he officially had to let his oldest daughter go off to start a family of her own. My grandad slowed down the pace and took a step every three seconds. In fact, he walked so slowly the piano had to repeat the tune over and over again. I don't know about anyone else in the church, but that song quickly stopped being my favorite after the third round. After two years, my mom finally met up with my dad in the front. I looked over to my dad and saw that he was teary-eyed.

After they exchanged vows, they each received their rings from one another and—the grossest part yet—they even kissed. Then they both received two jewelry boxes, one pink and gold, and the other purple and blue. I just knew which one was going to be handed to me because I'd always stressed how my favorite colors were pink and gold. Instead, they switched the boxes and I got the purple and blue box. I looked down at the box and looked back up, expecting an "oops, we accidentally mixed things up." I was an only child and I was used to things being fixed for me if they didn't turn out right. Today was my mom's day, though, so I would have to suck it up to keep from causing a scene. My dad proceeded to open my box, take a necklace out, and try to put it around my neck, but he couldn't because it was tangled. I looked over to my right to see my sister's necklace perfectly aligned on her neck as she exchanged a smile with my mom.

I looked back up to my dad and he gave me the "I don't know what else to tell you" stare. He took the tangled necklace and aligned it up on my neck with the tangled ends hanging off the back of my neck. I walked back with a frown to stand next to my sister in the bridesmaid line.

The wedding gave me assurance that not only did I cherish this man who I knew would treat my mom right, but he would also be the best dad to me and would complete our family. Till this day the necklace is still tangled after all of those years, but glancing at it every once in a while takes me back to this day when I felt such a strong sense of confirmation that my family was now complete. I've never seen my mom happier in my life. I smiled just as wide as she did, hoping we could make eye contact to share the moment.

She came down the aisle beaming with joy and met my dad and they shared their vows. When the wedding ended I knew this meant serious family business.

"I officially have a father and a sister," I thought to myself.

Jasmyne and my dad both taught me that family goes much deeper than being related by DNA, that it's about love. Between my dad and me, there was never a dull moment, so many jokes and laughs until I had tears in my eyes. And even though sisters can sometimes make you want to rip their heads off, Jasmyne took on the role of being my big sister and treated me like I was automatic family without hesitation. She gave me the best advice for my little third-grade friendship crisis, and she dried my tears the time I

cried over the ponytail my mom gave me because it wasn't high enough. We weren't even going anywhere that day, but whatever was a big deal to me, she never treated it as if it were any less important to her. I wonder how she didn't just laugh right in front of my face in moments like these, but she never did.

It wasn't until about five years after the wedding that I took into consideration that my last name does not match the rest of my family's last name. I was the only one out of the whole family whose last name was still Smith. I didn't know it at the time, but the longer I acted as if it weren't a big deal, the heavier it began to weigh on me. Deep inside I knew there was nothing wrong with not sharing last names—I always knew I was considered an Unseld at heart—but I wanted to be able to write it down on paper for class assignments and school documents. First I mentioned it to my mom. I didn't know how to tell my dad without it coming out as a command of, "I want my last name changed, now." This concern gradually grew a lump in the pit of my stomach.

After a regular, long, tiring school day, I walked home from the bus. My back ached because of the long walk to my house. The heat formed beads of sweat on my forehead as I strode all the way up the hill. I finally arrived at my house and collapsed on the couch with my legs weighing me down like anchors. I did not feel like being bothered with anyone. I had no energy to even turn on my favorite TV show, which was usually included in my after-school routine. I didn't feel like talking, moving, eating—nothing. I just sat there and watched the slow ceiling fan blow as little air as possible around and around and around. Eventually, I stirred up the strength to get up and go into the family room to start my homework. Right as I plopped down to start, my dad stood in front of me, projecting a warm smile in my direction as if he were expecting my presence. *He never just sits and smiles at me. This better not be another, "Aha, I gotcha" moment—I am definitely not in the mood.* I had no clue what he was up to. He slowly made his way towards me and handed me a crisp white paper. It was some sort of official letter and in fine print, it said "NATALIA UNSELD."

My eyes instantly filled with warm tears. I'd cried plenty of times during the course of my life, but these tears felt unfamiliar. These tears carried the weight of assurance and confirmation. I couldn't find the right words to express the joy that filled my spirit. I released all my emotion into a hug. We exchanged no words, but my heart excitedly beat against his chest.

Nothing was said, but everything was understood. It settled an uneasy feeling in my spirit that I had never really been able find the words to describe. It felt as if a lump in my throat that I'd been ignoring for years now had finally fallen and disappeared for good. I felt new as day.

"I'm official," I said. "This is finally official."

Lots of people were congratulating my family and me on the name change, but the person who mattered the most to me was Jasmyne. After a few days she called me. "Hey, Talia!" she said.

"Hey, Jazzy...." I paused, awaiting what I'd been expecting to hear from her for days now.

"I heard you got your name changed! How exciting. It's finally official now. I just want you to

know you've always been a sister to me no matter what, but *this*…this is special, this is some serious change. How do you feel?"

"I actually don't feel all that different," I said. "Like you said, it all felt real already. Now it's just on paper."

"Well, doesn't this mean you're technically adopted?" I could hear her joking voice slowly rise as she asked the question and I could see a sarcastic smile inching across her face through the phone.

"Haha, very funny." We both laughed almost to tears. We could only manage broken, unfinished words after that because of how hard we were laughing.

When my name first changed, it felt weird, almost uncomfortable. After seeing my name so many times on field trip forms and report cards, I was attached to the name *Smith*. Even though it was

associated with memories I wasn't too fond of, it still belonged to me. It was my title. While writing my name on my paper in class, I thought to myself, *Smith is really gone, it's actually official: no more Smith*. It took months to feel completely comfortable writing my new last name. Though I was excited at becoming an official *Unseld*, a part of the old Natalia was still processing all of this. After I grew comfortable with writing "Unseld" without it feeling like a foreign language, I was able to slowly take in everything happening around me. I realized the power that a name holds. It truly does become a big part of your identity.

My relationship with my dad has not only brought new insight into my life, but also relationships with new people I could never have imagined meeting, most importantly Jasmyne. Though we have had countless arguments over who stole what from whom, or who was copying whom, she has truly taught me what family actually means. Jasmyne has shown me you can still be sisters even if it's not in the traditional way. She's proven to me that I can still depend on her for just about anything.

Today it feels like this is the way it should have always been. When I say "Happy Father's Day" I have no confusion as to who I am talking to. Family is bound not by blood, but through love. Every day he reminds me of how important it is to have a father figure in my life. Motivating me to be the best Natalia I can be. He will always be more than deserving of the title Father to me.

PHOTO BY KERTIS CREATIVE

PAOLA
JIMENEZ MORA

WHEN YOU PLANT AN ORANGE TREE

Five days a week, my sister Maria, my boxer Camu, and I used to wait for my dad to come home from work at 6 p.m. We had played all day from one side of our family property in the countryside of Costa Rica to the other without a single care or worry. Camu's tongue hung outside his mouth from the fatigue. The three of us always sat in the same place on the ground, admiring the sky changing from purple to orange to yellow until night fell, our family land attached to our bodies.

We always enjoyed the same routine. My sister waited for my dad after work with clothes and a bath towel because she wanted to make everything easier and faster for him, so that he would not waste time and have the whole night for us two. We were anxious to hug him. When he kissed us, his beard—a little one, like a teenager's—would tickle us and make us laugh. Our dad has an intimidating, muscular appearance, but a gentle, sweet, sentimental personality. He bites his lip when he is stressed and talks to his belly as if he were pregnant when he is nervous. He is friendly, one of those who makes jokes at everything to make others laugh. He is a magician and juggler, and sometimes even a tightrope walker. When he played with us, he was whatever we wanted him to be:

a superhero, a queen, a rock star, our manager, our customer, our teacher. He created stories that nobody knew, and was able to repeat them almost word for word the next night. Being a father was never a task for him. Rather, it was an art. Everything looked prettier being his daughters, and laughter was more sincere, more enjoyable. My dad always made it clear to us that if he had to, he would give his own life for me and my sister. He would give it more than once if he could.

One day when I was nine years old, I came home from school like I normally did and my whole family was in the house. It was normal for my mother to be there with my sister and my grandmother who lived next door, but my father? Normally at that time of day he was at work. Even more strange, but exciting, my paternal grandparents were at my house during the week. I ran into my father's arms as always. He always said, "If you're not going to give me a bear hug, then don't hug me." But this time, his bear hug was stronger and longer than every one he had given me before. My sister was four years old and I was nine; maybe because of our age, my family didn't tell us what was happening. Clearly something was wrong, but how was I supposed to know what?

My paternal grandmother was on her knees praying to the Virgin Mary. "Cúbrelo con tu manto divino, Madre. Eres madre y sabes lo que siento." *Cover him with your divine mantle, Mother. You are a mother and you know what I feel.* She knew that what my father was going to go through was not nice, that it was illegal, and that he could go to jail for it. She could not do anything for him but sit down, cry, and pray to her God.

My uncles took us out to the playhouse my dad had built for us so we weren't in the house when all the mess was going on. I heard my mom crying and crying. I saw each of my family member's faces in slow motion. My mom did not usually show emotions, but that day there was nothing that would bring joy back to her face, to her life; that day she did not radiate light as she used to do. She looked lost.

At nightfall, my father left. I didn't know that I would have to get used to not seeing him every morning, and that I would not have his good night kiss or his arms to fall asleep in when my insomnia arrived.

My father built our house with his own hands on my grandmother's land where many people in the family lived. That house was our safe place where he imagined his daughters would grow up. If you asked my house to speak, she would tell you about the first time I read a book and the first time I wrote under her roof. She would tell you every joke my father told, and no matter how senseless it was, how it made us laugh. She would talk about each of my father's caresses of my mother. She would remember the smells of each of the meals my parents created for us.

That house kept all the good night stories that my father invented for us. She kept all of the mischief my sister and I did, like moving a chair so we could reach sweets that we were not supposed to eat at that time of morning.

For all of us who come from "third world countries" like Costa Rica, "first world countries" like the U.S. are always synonymous with money, well-being, and a better future. That was how my father saw it before he immigrated. My father left Costa Rica to work in the U.S. so that he could pay the debt he had with the bank after he borrowed some money to build our house. He built that house with his own hands so that we didn't have to pay rent anymore, so that we would have a place in the world that belonged to us, and we lived there, united and warm. But things got out of his hands, which never happened because my father planned for everything. He didn't see it coming, though. My father did the calculations, and the money he made would not be enough to repay the loan. If he didn't pay, the bank would take our home as payment. He knew that working in the United States would be an easy way to repay the loan so that we could keep our home and get on with our lives as they were before: happy, together, loving each other.

The next morning, the house did not smell like his cologne. My father was not the one who woke me up at five in the morning to prepare me for school. There was not a cup of cereal served on my table. He used to make it with warm milk and sugar, and he was the only one who knew how to do it. It took me three weeks to realize that he would not come back. My mother didn't explain it; she never talked to me about my father, and I never asked her about him. Maybe my mother was depressed because of my father's

departure, or maybe not. But we went shopping at the mall and she bought dresses, shoes, hats, bags, and perfumes. Then one day about a week after Dad left, my mom was seated at the coffee table, signing a bunch of papers and smiling. It was something about the house. My father had just left the country to earn money to pay for our house, but my mother sold our home and many of the things that were inside it. We never took anything from my home. Not my bed or my clothes or my toys. Nothing. We just left with a little suitcase. We stopped going to school. It was like vacation, but I didn't know that we were never coming back to the house. My home—my safe place—would belong to someone else and my family would never be the same.

We moved from hotel to hotel for three or four days at a time. The hotels usually would not have enough light coming through the window. The room colors were not creative, they didn't even try. Everything looked like a green vomit. They were definitely not family hotels: no swimming pools, green spaces, or children around. It was just me and my sister in these rooms, everything so very quiet. We only saw my mother at night, way after our bedtime. I never felt so alone as those nights we spent there.

My sister played with whatever she had in front of her. She built a house with all of the pillows in the room. The TV remote control became her pretend phone which she used to call my dad. She told him things like: "Hi, Daddy. Yes, we're fine. Yes, I miss you too. I love you so much. Come here, sleep with me, okay. Bye, I love you. Okay, bye, I love you more." Over and over again. She sometimes shouted that conversation, sometimes whispered it. Other times

she said it so fast that what she ended up forming was a tongue twister. But she never changed what she said. She always expected him to come through that hotel room door. I spent so much time sitting on the floor under a bedside table because I didn't want my sister to see me cry. I felt cold, I felt fear, I felt craving, I felt hate. My mother leaving us there alone made me feel that she hated us. But I hated even more that my father was not there.

I believed that my mother was not interested in me or my sister, or that my father had left the country to take care of us. What did she have in her head? I thought parents knew what things you weren't supposed to do. I had to take a role that a nine-year-old girl should not have to. I had concerns that were a little bigger than the concerns I had a month before. I went from feeding my grandparents with make

believe meals—soups made of river water, tamales made of mud, stones as meat, the leaves of the trees as our plates, and juice made of water colored with squeezed flowers—to feeding my sister with whatever was in the fridge, whether I knew how to cook or not. We had to eat. I gave my food to her because what we had was not enough for her to be full, and I filled her head with stories that my father had created for us and told us until we fell asleep. I told her about every special meal that my mother cooked differently for each of us so that my sister wouldn't grow up with a grudge like the one I was growing and kept for a long time.

I don't remember asking my mom, "Where is Dad?" They never talked about it. To this day, I don't like to talk about this stuff with my family. Every time I ask them about it, my dad has one side that he never fully explains and my mom has another side and she doesn't ever explain. My dad was never a really loving person with my mom. She likes to be one person's priority. She likes nice things. She likes when someone tells her, "You look beautiful today" or, "The food is absolutely delicious and you're really good at this." My dad never gave that to her, and I think she was a really lonely person. Probably my dad and my mom were not meant to be. She was going through a lot of stuff, and she found a person that she probably felt she was meant to be with, so she just went for it without even caring what would happen to us.

After the hotels, we went to a new place. We woke up in a house where the rooms were happier. Lots of light came in through the windows. After a few minutes of waiting seated on the bed, some children came into the room and shouted, "Abuela, the oldest one woke up!" The room filled up with people with new and strange faces, mostly children who were nice to us. The place was nice. There were many animals and that made me happy, at least for a moment. That's the day I saw my mother holding hands with a man who was clearly not my father. I did not like seeing him near my mother, near me, or near my sister.

My mom's "boyfriend's" family home house was isolated from the city, sat on a gravel road, and was surrounded by a lot of nature. A small river ran in front of the house, and the children, with the help of their grandfather, had made a "river pot" to swim in, which made it so exotic and exciting. While we swam in the river I forgot my worries. Finally, a happy place. We played in the river all day then went inside when night fell because of coyotes near the river.

The house smelled of food, smelled of home, smelled like what my life had been before. After we ate, the children took all their toys to the living room. We spent a long time there until my mother arrived. After that, something happened that continues to hurt ten years later. I still don't know how she found us—we were on the whole other side of the country—but my dad's sister came to that house and screamed at my mom. My mother and aunt had always gotten along but that day they talked to each other as if they were strangers who hated each other. My aunt yelled at my mother and my mother answered in the same way. My mother shouted that she was our mother and that no one had the right to take us away from her. My aunt shouted that giving birth was not the same as being a mother. She said that a mother was the one who took care of her kids, a mother is the one who wants good for her kids before herself, and that causing suffering to her kids did not make her an exemplary mother but a weak one. My sister had her little hands in her mouth; she cried and her body was trembling. We had reached a point where our own family caused us fear.

My aunt came with the police, and that day we learned that each action has a reaction in the worst way we could learn it. My mother's bad actions brought one of the most painful reactions of my life: they took my sister and me to the Patronato Nacional de la Infancia—the National Childhood Board, or PANI. For about a week we lived in a home with a bunch of kids who didn't have families while they looked for my dad. Most of them were about five years old. I was ten, and the oldest. At the time there were no cell phones and so there was no way to contact my dad. I couldn't imagine being a kid without a family, but the

kids living there didn't have anyone, just the people who were working there, and they were not nice.

After about a week, my sister and I had a meeting at the PANI office to decide if we were going to leave my mom and stay with my dad. PANI was supposed to be a friendly organization that worked for children. For me, it was like going to a haunted house. On the outside it had a bright yellow color but it did not transmit life: it transmitted anxiety. The short security guard at the front door was very friendly, and not even the gun he had hanging on his waist was scarier than seeing my mother's long face.

She knew that what would come next was not good.

The waiting room had sad, orange curtains and cold, green chairs that were a little high for kids. My feet swayed from one side to the other because they didn't touch the floor. There were toys to distract you so you would not realize what was happening, but that was not me that day. The toy houses looked old and dull, the dolls looked disheveled. The green areas needed the hands of grandmothers to give them life with flowers that only they knew how to plant and maintain. The soil in a potted plant was gray where some child had watered it with milk.

There were mothers on one side and children on the other. No one spoke. All I heard was children, crying, maybe singing a little. They were sleepy, hungry, or maybe afraid. I smiled so my sister would do it too and then everything would be good for her. Each of the social workers had a separate room, but you could hear what was happening in the room next to you, and believe me, you didn't want that.

My mother said that there were only female social workers because women were more sensitive than men and that was good for children. That made no sense to me, though, because I had my father as an example of a man, and he is the most sensitive, loving person I have ever met. My father's mother and sister had their turn first. My grandmother had a red face; her blood pressure was high. Her voice was very strong; the words that came out of her mouth hurt, and the wounds they left would not heal with a band aid. My aunt told my mother she was a bad mother and a bad wife, and that she didn't deserve to have my sister and me live with her. My grandmother and my aunt treated my mother as a bad mother in front of me. I knew they loved me and that they were worried about me.

My mother was someone who always looked straight ahead, but that day she had her head down all day. Her face was full of guilt, and she was not wearing makeup to cover her wrinkles. Before that day the lines in her face had expressed joy, but that day they expressed regret. She was going to lose us.

I was nine years old, so the law said I could choose who to be with: my mother or my grandparents. Can you imagine a nine-year-old girl having such a decision in her hands? *Do I leave my sister and choose to stay with my mother while she keeps partying? Or do I leave her all alone, become a bad daughter, and go wait at my grandparents' house until my father arrives?* I didn't want to lose my mother and I didn't want to be separated from my sister. My sister was only four and she could not choose; she was going to stay with my mom no matter what.

That day I decided to leave my mother and my sister too. I thought I was "making the best decision," but why did I feel so bad? I was the one who taught my sister to read and write. I was kind of like her mom figure, but now I was leaving her. I felt that I had destroyed the family.

No one in my family ever sat me down and talked with me about what was going on. Ever. I only knew what was going on because I overheard my grandma and my aunts and uncles talking about it. Whenever I felt bad, my grandpa tried to make me feel better. He was always playing his guitar and singing, telling jokes and stories that he made up. They lived close to a river, and my uncles took me swimming, played soccer with me, and played music for me. My grandma loved to cook and every day she cooked me everything I wanted. Like arepas, corn tortillas that look like pancakes but taste better. At night, we didn't have cable to watch movies, so my uncle who writes songs would use his imagination for our entertainment. He would act out all the parts of a movie like *Sleeping Beauty*. Everything was nice at my grandparents' house for the first few weeks. It felt like a Christmas trip. My grandparents slept next to me, my uncles and aunt were there, I had a lot of very nice attention from my family.

Not only did I not have the material things that others had, I did not have the family that others had.

While my grandparents were very good to me from the day I arrived, they were also very rude when it came to talking about my mother, and that hurt me. Maybe they didn't know it because I never said it, but I was afraid to speak. How could I oppose them if they took care of me? I had to reinvent a completely new life: new town, new school, new friends. I no longer had my mother or father next to me. I didn't have my bed anymore. I had no one to tie my laces. I had no one to do my hair before going to school like my dad used to do. I did not have my sister next to me every night when I slept, and that was what hurt most. My sister had a habit of touching my face in the middle of the night just to be sure I was there next to her, and now? I was not there, no matter how much I wanted to be. I felt so guilty for leaving Maria, like I was the worst sister. I was not there to cover her and make her feel comfy. I wasn't there in the morning to make cereal. Who would heat the milk for her if I wasn't there? Who would be her adventure partner? Who would teach her everything I already knew? Who would make her feel safe and capable of anything? I knew that was not going to be me.

After a while, certain attitudes changed at my grandparent's house. My paternal grandmother is one of the people who does not necessarily have an open mind, and as a child she experienced many things that she did not deserve. She has always been a giving person, but many times she demonstrated love in a way that hurt, perhaps because that was the definition of love that she knew. My grandmother grew up under a roof where the woman was synonymous with serving the man, so the duties she did at her home were "basic things that all women must know how to perform." I had to learn how to make rice, how to light a wood stove, how to wash and fold laundry, how to clean. She saw it as normal because it was what she grew up with. I didn't see it as normal, but at that point in my life I had no choice but to get used to it and to understand that it was the life that I had to live. Living under her roof, I didn't have time to act like a girl.

For a few months I had no communication with my sister, my mother, or my father. Then my mom gave my sister to our grandmother, saying that my sister needed me next to her. She showed up with Maria and said, "Maria no puede estar sin su hermana. Adios." *Maria can't be without her sister. Goodbye.* And then she left, and Maria and I lived with my grandmother together without knowing much about my parents until the day my father returned from the United States when I was thirteen years old.

That day we woke up a little earlier than normal, but it didn't matter because my father was finally coming home. My family rented a huge van big enough to hold all fifteen of the people who wanted to have my father next to them once again and making them smile. I had never traveled to the capital, nor had I been to an airport. Four hours of travel, four hours of seeing my grandmother biting her nails because, she said, of the "emotion." Four hours of listening to my uncles, grandfather, and great-grandfather sing songs that made them happy and made the time pass faster. My aunt wore sunglasses so no one would see her cry. I spent every second thinking about what it would be like to hug him again. I didn't know what to say. I didn't know how to act. I didn't know if he had changed. I was afraid. I was anxious. I had questions. I would no longer have to close my eyes at night to hear his voice. I would not cry anymore thinking that he was cold or hot or going hungry. I knew that the problems that had caused his departure would begin to have a solution.

It was strange to see my father again after so long without communication with him. He had gained a lot of weight. For five years he had worked thirteen hours a day, seven days a week in a country that was not his. Five years of hating having made the decision to leave us behind, of deciding not to call because he'd cry if he heard our voices. Five years of believing he was a bad father who couldn't take his daughters to school or help us with our homework, five years without good night kisses, without bear hugs while lying on the floor, without a "Te amo, Papi."

We had no place to live other than in my grandmother's house, but according to my father it was going to be temporary. He got a job at a hardware store so we could move out of my grandma's and rent a place where the three of us could live together again, but that never happened. My dad had changed a lot. He was depressed after leaving for the United States with a house in his name and returning to Costa Rica empty-handed and divorced. My father decided to drown his sorrows in alcohol. He drank every single day after work and would totally change. We began to fear our own father when he was under the influence.

If he was really mad he would fight with my uncles. My uncles would say, "You have to stop. You cannot be drinking in front of your kids. They are crying and afraid of you." My dad would say, "You can't tell me what to do!" and they'd fight like they were enemies, which was really scary. Other times he was calm and quiet and would just come home and cry and say, "I'm sorry. I don't want to be mean anymore. You don't deserve it. I'm not a good person. Your mom doesn't even love me anymore because I'm not enough." I was scared for him because I didn't remember him being like that before he left. I remembered my dad being the best person I had ever known, a peaceful and happy and loving person.

Economically, we were not well off. Even though my father worked to survive, to live day to day, we ate beans if we were lucky. We cooked our food on a wood stove. I could not have many of the things I wanted or felt I needed to fit into my group of friends at school. Many times they pushed me aside for not having the shoes that were in style at the moment, or not having the perfume that our favorite singer had created. My clothes were really old and secondhand. Not only did I not have the material things that others had, I did not have the family that others had. I didn't have Sundays together, I didn't have movie nights, or evenings where everyone cooked together and sat at their table to talk about their days. I cried at night, asking God to reunite my family again, to be fair to me and my sister.

There were still some good times, though. There was a house up the road where a few kids lived and sometimes we would play with them. When my dad wasn't drinking he would take us all to the river and we would swim all day. We were like fish.

Swimming was our thing. After we went to the river we would eat fresh fruit. My grandpa had so much fruit growing on the land: mangoes, coconuts, bananas, strawberries, grapes. Sugar cane also grew all around my grandparents' place and I would eat it fresh all day. It's the best.

Years passed and I was no longer that girl who feared her own family. My mentality had changed, and I wanted to have my mother and her family close to me too. I wanted my dad to have a good relationship with my mother so that I could have a good relationship with her. As long as my parents didn't understand that their problems affected all of us, we weren't going to have a healthy relationship. My grandma had always told me that there were papers from the court that said our mom couldn't come close to us and that if she did, they could send her to jail.

My grandma told everybody at my school that my mom wasn't allowed to be at the school. We had a really small town and everybody knew about everybody's lives. One day we were playing at recess, and my friends started screaming, "Look! It's your mom! It's your mom!" And I was like, "Really?" I started shaking and lost my voice. *If she comes here, the police are gonna be here, then my grandma's gonna be here, and then it's gonna be a huge mess.*

My mom was holding a baby. I saw her through the fence. She walked up and said, "Hi, baby. Look, it's your brother."

I said, "I haven't seen you for a really long time and now I have a brother?" My grandma had told my mom that we didn't want to see her. "We really want to," I said, "but Grandma says that you cannot even be close because you can go to jail." Mom told me that the papers my grandma had told us about never existed. She made this whole story up because she was afraid that we would be close to my mom and then we would leave her after everything she had done for us.

So I started to see my mom on Saturdays for a few hours. Then we would go back to my grandmother and the routine would repeat itself. She was always saying that my mom was a really bad person and she couldn't understand why I wanted to see her. But I never saw my mom as the bad person in the story. I thought I was in the way at my grandparents' house, and I did not want to continue living in a house where they reminded me that, thanks to them, I did not live on the street. My grandma is a really kind and lovely person. Everybody who knows her loves her. But she can also be really difficult. I told my dad, "If you want me to stay with you, we have to move out. I love my grandma but she is not my mom. I know she has done so much for us, but we have to move out." My dad was like, "Yeah, we will. But I don't have the money right now. You have to do whatever your grandma says because we need to be here." It was really hard.

Then one day my mom planned a birthday party for herself, and my sister and I were going to go. The night before, my sister cleaned her shoes and laid out her best outfit on a chair close to her bed. Early the next morning we got ready and were about to leave and my grandma said, "Where are you guys going?"

"To Mom's," I said.

"No, you're not," she said. My sister started crying. We had been waiting the whole night and we wanted to be there with them.

"We're going," I said.

"Nope, you're not, because this is my house and these are my rules," she said.

Then I just started running. I was the one who fed all my grandma's animals—the chickens and dogs and horses—and they were all following me as I ran across the farm. My sister cried and said, "Don't leave me!"

We lived in the forest, way too far away from the city where my mom lived. I ran to the first house I came to and asked to use their phone. I called my mom. I was crying and said to her, "Can you come and pick me up? I don't want to live with my grandma anymore."

She came in a cab and took me to her house. It was this huge house, a really nice place. My stepfather Richard is an American architectural engineer, and they had money.

The days passed and the relationship with my mother was a little strange. She had her new family, so my idea of seeing my parents back together would remain just an idea in my head. I did not want to have contact with my father because the calls he made were drunk, crying, and asking for forgiveness. I did not want to have contact with my father's family because I was afraid that my grandma would say that I just wanted to live with Mom and Richard because they had money and that all I cared about was money and having a really good life. That wasn't true. I just felt like I needed my mom in my life at that time. But I felt that I had been ungrateful when I left the house that had saved me from living on the street.

I was thirteen when I moved back to my mom's. I was still going to school. In order to be in Costa Rica without permanent residency, my stepdad had to leave every three months for thirty days, and then he could come back to Costa Rica. The whole month he was gone, my mom would start going to parties again, and I would be the one who took care of my brother. Once, she left on a Wednesday, and didn't come back for almost a week. I missed a whole week of school because I had to take care of my two-year-old brother. I stopped doing my homework. I thought, *I'm not going to be able to finish school*. At fifteen I stopped attending school.

The relationship with my mother was not good, so I went back and forth between my mom's and my grandma's several times in those years. My grandma would say, "See. I told you your mom is a really bad person. She doesn't care about you. She only cares about her friends and parties and really nice outfits. She only wants you there because she needs a babysitter. She doesn't care if you go to school." I started to believe all of that.

But I wanted to take care of my brother because my mom was not really a good mom. I needed to make sure that he was eating and reading books. All the stuff I had done with my sister Maria, I thought I should do with him.

Then one day Maria called my mom crying, saying she did not want to be with Dad and Grandma anymore. So she moved back in with our mom and stepdad too. It had been three years since we had lived in the same house. I spent days showing her the world outside my grandparents' house that she didn't know. We ate things that we never had at my grandparents'. I took her to buy clothes in a large shopping center. We each had a room of our own that we could decorate according to our taste, but we slept in the same bed together anyway. My mom said, "The whole point of having your own rooms is that you can sleep in your own beds." And I said, "Nope." Finally Maria and I were together again, and I didn't need anything else.

One day were having lunch and my mom was on Facebook. She saw that her friend was living in the U.S. I jokingly said, "Let's go to the U.S." My mom said, "Do you want to move to the U.S.?" I was like, "Yeah, why not?" When we talked to my stepdad, he said, "You really want to leave? You realize that I'm living here because I like it here. My country is really cold, and I have the beach here and it's very tropical. You want me to move one more time to my country? I can have my job no matter where I live. I have all I need. But if your future is not here, if you feel like you want to go over there, you have to make a promise: never stop going to school, and get your diplomas."

I hadn't gone to school in four years at that point, and going back to school was never the plan for me. My plan was to come to the U.S. and work. If I had to be a housekeeper with my mom, then I would do it. I thought only of my brother and sister and the opportunities they would have there. When I thought about leaving Costa Rica, it didn't seem like it would be very different. I was living with my family. I never had a bunch of friends or a social life outside my house. The big difference would be that I would be in another country and I wouldn't have my grandma or my dad close to me.

When we called my dad and told him we were trying to go live in the U.S., he told us, "No, you cannot do this. You already live too far away from me. We barely see each other, and if you go to the U.S., it's gonna be impossible for me to see you." My dad was in the U.S. for four years illegally. It is hard to come back after that.

"You are working just to live and pay your bills," I said. "You can't go shopping too much because you won't be able to pay your bills. I don't want my sister and my brother to have this life." In Costa Rica, you have to be a really good doctor or a lawyer to be able to live well and take vacations. If you don't have a diploma it is really hard to get a good job. You are only working to live day by day. I didn't want that life for my sister and my brother. "Our stepdad is giving us this opportunity, where my sister can go learn another language and get a diploma and go to an American university. We are not going to get another opportunity like this one. Just because we'll be living in another country doesn't mean you are going to stop being our dad. You just have to think about what a good opportunity this is for us. We are not going to be illegal. We'll have residency. This might not ever happen again."

He thought about it and said, "You're right. I want you to be happy. Go ahead."

I arrived in the United States about two years ago without a plan, without knowing what to do. I had not been to school since eighth grade, more than five years. I had never been to high school. I didn't know anything about math. I had no idea that y = mx + b. I didn't know who Newton was or why he was important. I didn't know anything about history. I was lost. After attending the Newcomer Academy for six months, I arrived at Central High School in 2018. There were many obstacles in the classroom. I didn't speak the language. If they said one hundred words, I was lucky to understand forty. My classmates did not speak to me because I think they just did not know if I was able to understand them.

When I arrived in the United States, I didn't fit in and I didn't understand stereotypes. I didn't know that if you are Latino you are a bad person and a drug dealer. I didn't know that all Latinos had caramel dark skin. I didn't know all Latinos had to dance. I didn't know all Latinos like spicy food or that we are loud and dramatic. It is so difficult to make people understand the opposite, to make them understand that we are more than that. But what hurt me the most was my age. I was now twenty-one years old. I was a senior in high school. I didn't yet have a degree from a place where you usually leave when you're seventeen. People looked at me like I was an idiot. "What are you doing here still? Why are you not in college? You can already drink alcohol! You can leave your home without asking permission!" Their comments made me lose faith in myself, made me ashamed of myself. The nights before school, I cried silently and deeply. I was disgusted with myself. Stress was damaging me, not only mentally, but physically. I developed ulcers and spent two days in the hospital. When I got out, I decided to abandon my studies again. There was just no way for me to be a "normal high school girl," and I thought I could never get my high school diploma.

My family wasn't happy with me, but they never said anything about it, maybe because when I arrived in the United States the plan was that I would work. A month passed, and the subject of my returning to school had not been touched upon until my ESL teacher, Ms. Morris, sent a letter to my house through my sister. She asked me to come back. She believed in me more than I did. My counselor called my house

the future she had wanted to give me but at the time was not possible—it was more than enough.

When I came back, it was so difficult. All my grades were U's, and I knew that I didn't have much time. I knew that second chances are rare, and that I had to take advantage. Six months later, I was on the honor roll, I was president of the Spanish Club, and I was a member of the National Honor Society and the Beta Club. Believing in myself—believing with hurricane strength—took me to places I hadn't known were attainable.

It is a Costa Rican tradition to "darle honor a tu apellido," which means *give honor to your last name*. I had to make my family proud. I have always wanted a future that will shine so much that it will fill my parents' faces with pride. But I didn't do it just for my family. I did it for me. I wanted to see that if I wanted something I could do it. It was really hard, especially in the pandemic, because if I don't have a teacher in front of me it's really hard to understand English assignments. On top of that, I was working sixty hours a week, I was helping my dad by sending a little money, and I was helping my mom clean houses on the side. But I did it. I got my diploma. I have work now and my own apartment, and I'm paying my own bills.

The day we left Costa Rica, Maria and I were in my dad's car on the way to the bus station. Nobody said a word. We couldn't even look at each other's faces. Then Dad stopped the car. He turned to us and said, "You know that you two are the greatest thing I have ever done. I have made so many mistakes, but God really must love me because look at you two. You're just perfect. I have done something really good in my life to have you guys. I'm always gonna

and asked me to return. My stepfather was the one at that time who convinced me to get in his car and to go to school once again. He let me know that life was always going to be uphill, but that the view from the top would be wonderful. He told me we had come to this country to take the opportunity to study here.

When I saw Ms. Morris in the counselor's office, I couldn't hide my tears. My only reaction was to hug her. No one had ever made me feel more capable. My mother cried when she saw me cry, and my stepfather cried when he saw us cry. I had never been so happy to be in the right place with the right people. Since the day that I met her, Ms. Morris has inspired me, and she continues to do so with each action. Seeing my mother looking towards me with a smile and hope on her face again because she knew that I could have the future she had wanted but could not have, be proud of you. I don't care if you have a diploma or not. I don't care what you plan to do with your life. I don't care if you get married, if you never get married, if you have children, if you never have children. I'm always gonna be proud of you.

"Listen, you're gonna be over there and it's gonna be really hard. That's not your country, and that's not your culture, and that's not your language. There will be people who think they are better than you. But never forget that you have come really, really, far to get over there, and they don't know what you've been through. You always have to remember that what a person gives to you is what they have. If a person is very mean to you it's because they have pain in their life; that's not the way they want to treat you. If you plant an orange tree, you get oranges; you are not supposed to get apples."

That's the way I feel about my mom too. You give what you have. You do whatever you know. I've never wanted my mom to be another person. That's just the way she is. I once asked her, "Why aren't you like those moms in the movies? Like when you have a crush on somebody and you can go to your mom and say, 'Oh my God! I love this kid at school.' I've never talked to you that way." She said, "Because I never had that person. I don't know how to do it because nobody ever did that for me. I wasn't able to go to my mom because I was too busy being a wife." My mom and I love each other. I never hated on her. She got pregnant when she was twenty years old, and I think she wasn't ready to be a mom.

I always think that you are born to be something in your life. A good doctor, a good mother. I think she wasn't really meant to be a mom. There are people who are just not meant to be parents. I am trying to

Believing in myself—believing with hurricane strength—took me to places I hadn't believed were attainable.

become the person that I wanted my mom to be. The only thing in life that I really, really want is to have kids. I feel like I was meant to be a mom.

I think about the week that Maria and I spent in foster care. We were so sad. It was not fair for those kids to grow up without having a person who loves them the most. They didn't have hugs or hot cereal or stories at night or a kiss. Every single time they'd see a car coming they would all scream, "Oh my God! This could be us!" They were waiting for somebody to come and adopt them. Every single time a car came it was like, "This could be my opportunity to get out of here." That's the point when I realized that even though my grandma was really hard on me, and my mom was not there sometimes because she was partying, I was lucky. I had a family. Had a grandma and a mom and a dad. That's what it took for me to realize how lucky I was.

My grandpa used to tell me, "Dios tirar las peores batallas a mejores soldados." *God throws the worst battles at the best soldiers.* That's the way I see it. I feel like I had to live what I lived to get to the place I am right now. I would live it thousands of times again. I'm strong to be able to pass everything I did, to be the person I am today.

WITH THE VIRGEN DE LOS ÁNGELES

I had asked my father indirect questions about his emigration a few times and had talked with my mother and grandmother about it a little, but I'd never directly asked my dad what he'd been through. On my 21st birthday, September 5, 2019, I asked him to give me his story as a gift. I wanted to start my life as an adult by seeing him from another perspective. It hurt me to ask him to trace the days of pain he went through, but I needed to understand. After evading the issue, he finally told me, step by step, the events of the twelve days from when he left our house to when he arrived in the United States. He recorded the story on his phone and sent me the recording. Twelve minutes of him talking about those twelve days.

That was the point when I realized how much my dad loves me and my sister. He suffered for twelve days without us, without food or water. He did it for us. He had his life in Costa Rica. He had a house and a family that he left behind so that we could have a better future. It didn't work, of course, because of everything that happened. But he did that for us. I always thought that bad memories should not be remembered. But it turned out that my father needed to talk about it. In this way he was relieving himself of a story that was consuming him.

—Paola Jimenez Mora

The day I left the house, I took a plane to Mexico. I'd purchased a tourist package to the city of Monterrey to watch a game at the stadium. I was with a couple of other Costa Ricans, and when we landed in Mexico City we were detained because the consul at the airport took one look at us and assumed we were there to "pass to the other side." We spent six hours in that office without eating or drinking anything, and of course they had no proof of why we had traveled to Mexico. After a while they told us we could leave and to enjoy the game. From Mexico City we made one more plane trip to Monterrey, and when we arrived at the airport everything was fine. There was a bus waiting that took us to the stadium where we met up with two coyotes—those are people who are paid to transport migrants in secret. One of them was to take sixteen other migrants and the other was to take me, alone.

I spent the first half watching the game, then we went down from the stands to "buy something to eat." In reality we were waiting for some trucks that took us to a hotel where we checked in and waited till the next day for the same coyotes to pick us up. The other sixteen left in the morning with the one coyote, and I waited for mine until 8:00 a.m., but nobody arrived. No coyote came for me. I was in that hotel alone, alone, alone, alone, with a phone number that was written on the leg of my pants. I called and called but nobody ever answered. I waited in my room until the hotel staff came and told me that I had to leave because the hours I'd paid for the room had already expired. I was outside sitting at a public telephone when they finally answered my call. They told me to take a taxi to the bus station. The taxi driver was drinking alcohol, but I was going where I needed to go, so I couldn't say anything. At the bus station I had to buy a bus ticket that went from Monterrey to Nogales. If the trip had been direct, without any stops, it would have taken eighteen hours, but we were making stops: from Monterrey to Tepic, from Tepic to Culiacán, then Mazatlan, Sonora, Sonorita until reaching the U.S. border. They make those stops to eat, and I was so hungry, but I could not spend much money. I'd bought some tacos and a Coca Cola that lasted me all twenty-nine hours of travel.

The road was very long and lonely. I got on a bus, I got off to get on another, alone, without knowing anyone, without knowing anything, without knowing anybody, without knowing what bus was going to take me or where I was going. *Solo con Dios y La Virgen*, thinking of my daughters, my babies. How hard is this.

When I arrived in Sonora, a Mexican man from Michoacán came to meet me at the bus. He was white, short, had blue eyes, and wore a hat. He sat next to me and we started talking. "You're going to try, right?" he asked, which made me think he might be from La Migra, the immigration police. I told him that I was. The man told me to walk him to the bathroom. He could walk just fine, but he told me that he was going to act like it was hard for him, and that I was going to act like his grandson. We went down to the bathroom together and stayed in there while two officers were checking passports of people up on the bus. "When they leave," the man told me, "don't speak. I will answer for you. Just follow me." When we went back to the bus, an officer asked us for the papers, and the man told him that they were up on the bus. We got onto the bus to get the papers, but the doors closed and the bus continued on without any problem. So far, everything was going well. The man got off at the next stop and I was again as I came: alone. The man arrived in the place where I needed someone the most. An angel.

I arrived in Nogales. Everything looked deserted there. I took a taxi to the Hotel Jimenez and checked in. When I opened the door there were fifty or more people—Mexicans, Peruvians, Salvadorans, Hondurans, Nicaraguans—all waiting to be taken across the border. Fifteen people were on their way out, ready to go and try to cross the border. I went into the room and tried to accommodate myself. The sixteen Costa Ricans I had left with were there too. We talked for a while, and then someone brought us some nasty burritos. They threw them on the ground like we were animals. They threw them in our faces. They treated us like pigs. Before they left the room they screamed that they'd be back in three hours for fifteen more people. They would pick them up in cars and take them to a house in the desert where they'd wait for more people.

It was already night and I was falling asleep. I snore and make noises and they didn't want to hear it, so people threw whatever they had at me: wallets, sashes, shoes. I did not sleep that night. When my turn came, I went with fifteen Mexicans and two Costa Ricans. We were in the truck, and then we arrived at the house in the middle of the desert where they gave us some ramen noodle soup to eat. They gave us each a gallon of water and a bag with a pair of socks and a coat because at night it was cold. Then my group prayed together. The eldest Costa Rican had an image of the Virgin and he said to us, "Remember this. Remember this image perfectly in your mind. This is who will take you across the desert. She took me once." I did it, and I still have that image engraved in my mind so well. The image of La Virgen de los Ángeles.

At 1:27 a.m. they screamed to us that it was time to leave. They told us to run toward a spotlight where another coyote was waiting. We went out one by one, without stopping. At that time I said, *How easy. I am already in the U.S.* But it was not so. We walked for a while and then the cholos arrived and we were assaulted. Cholos are mestizo—white and indigenous—men who the coyotes tip off. They come and assault people who are making the crossing. They took our money and our pants, socks, jackets, and shoes. My shoes were not a known brand, so they didn't take mine, but one of them took fifty more dollars from me and said, "Thanks, wey. You're paying for the shoes I'm going to buy tomorrow." We walked all night without clothes, cold, and the others without shoes, but I had mine. How lucky was I, no?

We had to get under plastic at dawn in the desert because infrared airplanes passed overhead looking for people. We got under plastic every time a plane came. We walked a whole day more and then rested under some trees at nightfall. We continued walking until we reached a road that led to the state highway. There was a sewer, a very large tube, that we had to cross. It was twenty meters long and very dark. Once we were inside, patrols passed overhead. We continued walking and climbed a hill and went back down to a very dry river. We had to keep walking all day and night until we found a place where we could rest again. Then they assaulted us again. This time with weapons to our heads. I was lying next to the tree when I felt a gun to my head. They screamed at us to gather together and they assaulted us again. I had 100 dollars. My last 100 dollars with which I had to reach the United States. These men who assaulted us came with six Salvadorans, two of whom were women. One of them told me that if I had money to give it to her, that she could hide it in her hair. So I did. Some time passed and the coyotes raped them in front of everyone. They undressed them and they simply began to rape them in front of us. We couldn't do anything because they were drugged and the men were armed.

On the third day of walking, I couldn't do any more. I had no water. We had to look for water, and when we found some in a ditch it was full of frogs. We had to drink it like that—dirty and hot, with frogs and urine—but at least it was liquid. We arrived at a point in the desert where we were headed for La Migra. We had to go back to the sewer again. On the fourth day, after nightfall, they shouted at us that where the light was, that was the United States. We walked and walked and walked but the light never got closer. That day migration patrols on four-wheelers chased us. They took many of us that day. Next to me was a man named Juan. Juan de Cuernavaca. I couldn't go on anymore. My socks were full of blood. Blood pumped like glue from my socks. My lips were dry and split and bloody. Every time I had energy to, I walked with my heels. This man Juan grabbed my hand. "You are about to arrive," he said. But I couldn't go on. I closed my eyes and saw the Virgen de Los Ángeles that the old Costa Rican man had asked me to remember. I asked her for strength, more strength.

I was crying and the few tears that came out of my eyes came out hot. I was tired, asking for more strength, crying hot tears. Migration arrived and Juan told me to get on the ground and hide so that they would not grab me, but I didn't care anymore. I just wanted to drink water. Juan pushed me and I fell through a thicket and down a ravine. Then he was caught. I listened to the four-wheelers pass by me

and nobody saw me. They grabbed eight out of the twenty-six of us. Within minutes of being hidden, people began to leave the bush because they wanted water. They gave themselves up for water. I didn't. I had already come too far to give up. I stayed until I fell asleep. When I woke up, I was alone. God and the Virgin know that it is true. I got up and knew that if I followed the lights I would arrive. I took off my socks, full of blood, and put them on my hands. I left by myself and walked. I heard wolves, dogs, and horses in the background. I knew that if I arrived I would not know what to do. What would I do once I arrived if I had no one to call? I was alone.

I sat next to a tree. It was near dawn when I heard people in the distance. I came out so suddenly that they started shouting, "Immigration! Immigration!" but I said, "No, no. I am not. I need help." They gave me an orange and a sausage. You don't know how delicious that tasted. I still have that taste on my palate. They said that if I wanted to go with them, I had to run. After five days in a row of walking, I had to draw strength from where I didn't have any more. When the truck arrived, I fell. And these people, who had no idea if I was a good person or not, picked me up and threw me in the back of the truck.

They took me to a hotel. I locked myself in a room, closed my eyes, and cried. I thought of you, your sister, my mother, and your mother. In that moment I was back home in Peñas Blancas. I was next to you. I was back in the mornings when I would take you to school and you would tell me, "Don't leave, Daddy. I'm afraid. I need you here." And now I really was gone. You needed me, and I was not there anymore. I was crying in a room in the middle of LA with no answers to all the questions I had.

ACKNOWLEDGMENTS

An intensive and long-lasting project like this book is no small affair to organize and complete. It required the support of an entire community of individuals and organizations who believe in LSP's mission to amplify unheard voices and untold stories.

We would like to offer our most heartfelt thanks.

To the authors' families: Your children have done something remarkable here. With your support and guidance, they have given something truly important to a community who needs them and their voices so much right now. They could not have done it without you. Thank you.

To Ann Walsh: Your dedication to the students of Central High, your integrity, and your humanity are baked into these pages. It's impossible to imagine how this book could have come to light without your support and wise counsel. Thank you.

To Central High School and Principal Raymond Green: It has been an honor to conduct this project at Central and to play some small role in the story of an institution that is so significant to our city. Thank you for supporting LSP and the authors as we completed this work.

Shellee Marie Jones: We pinch ourselves every time we put your name in the acknowledgments of another book. We're so grateful to have worked with you again, each and every time. Thank you.

Kertis Creative: As you've helped to tell LSP's story over the years, you've also helped us understand our mission with greater focus. Your thoughtfulness is contagious. Thank you.

Norman Spencer: Thank you for coming aboard to create such a spectacular and moving cover for this book. It's perfect.

To our colleagues and the administration at Spalding University: Thank you for your support of LSP's work and for helping us carve out a home at Spalding.

To Louisville Nature Center for loaning computers to two of the authors when the pandemic hit.

Thank you to the major sponsors of this project: the Fund for the Arts, the C. E. and S. Foundation, the Norton Foundation, Louisville Metro Government, the Cralle Foundation, Mrs. Christina Lee Brown, Matthew Barzun & Brooke Brown Barzun, the Arthur K. Smith Family Foundation, and Owsley Brown III.

Thanks also to everyone else who provided funding for this project or general operating support, including: the Kentucky Arts Council, Porter Watkins & George Bailey, Emily Bingham & Stephen Reily, Mimi Zinniel, Clarese Fuller, Rick & Corie Neumayer, Ted & Mary Nixon, the Kentucky Colonels, Allen Bush & Rose Cooper, Phil & Landis Thompson, the Rajon Rondo Foundation, Susan Bentley, Gladys Lopez, Lynn Wilkinson, James & Vandy Chisholm, Yvette Gentry, Nina Bonnie, Kristen Lucas, Doug Churchman (Class of '90), Valle Jones, the LG&E Foundation, Anne McKune, M.A. & Ed Allgeier, Luke Boyett, Graham & Martha Neal Cooke, Lori Hudson Flanery, Claudia Gentile, Bob & Bo Manning, Jean Baker Mansfield, Janice Pullen (USAF, ret.), Ellen Sears, Michelle Wells, Kathleen Woolridge, Gary & Carol George, Ann Coffey, Emmanuel Collins, Kate Lacy Crosby, Keith Look & Carlotta Kustes, Beth & Doug Peabody, Tom & Jenny Sawyer, Beth Bissmeyer, Cassiopia Blausey, Kat & Zack Conover, Dr. M. Denise Franklin-Williams, Jay Gulick & Mary Oliver Humke, Maria Gurren, Wendy LaTour-Marone, Judy & Fred Look, the Sachs family, Susan Woodcock & David Tachau, and Daryle & Cecily Unseld.

Thank you, reader, for purchasing this book and reading these important stories which the authors worked so hard on.

—Joe Manning, Elizabeth Sawyer, and Darcy Thompson
Louisville Story Program